D0975691

WOMEN, WORK
& THE ART
of
SAVOIR FAIRE

ALSO BY MIREILLE GUILIANO

French Women for All Seasons

French Women Don't Get Fat

WOMEN, WORK
& THE ART
of
SAVOIR FAIRE

Business Sense & Sensibility

MIREILLE GUILIANO

ATRIA BOOKS

NEW YORK   LONDON   TORONTO   SYDNEY

ATRIA BOOKS
A Division of Simon & Schuster, Inc.
1230 Avenue of the Americas
New York, NY 10020

Copyright © 2009 by Mireille Guiliano

All rights reserved, including the right to reproduce this book or portions thereof in any form whatsoever. For information address Atria Books Subsidiary Rights Department, 1230 Avenue of the Americas, New York, NY 10020

First Atria Books hardcover edition October 2009

ATRIA BOOKS and colophon are trademarks of Simon & Schuster, Inc.

For information about special discounts for bulk purchases,
please contact Simon & Schuster Special Sales at 1-866-506-1949
or business@simonandschuster.com.

The Simon & Schuster Speakers Bureau can bring authors to your live event. For more information or to book an event contact the Simon & Schuster Speakers Bureau at 1-866-248-3049 or visit our website at www.simonspeakers.com.

Designed by Jaime Putorti

Manufactured in the United States of America

10   9   8   7   6   5   4   3   2   1

Library of Congress Cataloging-in-Publication Data

Guiliano, Mireille, date.
    Women, work, and the art of savoir faire: business sense and sensibility / Mireille Guiliano.
        p. cm.
Includes index.
1. Businesswomen. 2. Success in business. I. Title.
    HD6053.G84 2009
    650.1082--dc22
                                                           2009011694

ISBN: 978-1-4165-8919-8
ISBN: 978-14165-9249-5 (ebook)

sa·voir faire \, sav-ˌwär-ˈfer\ *n.m.* **1:** Know-how. French *savoir-faire*, literally, knowing (*savoir*) how to do (*faire*). **2:** Competence, experience. **3:** The ready knowledge of the right course of action: knowing what to do and say and when and how to do so. **4:** *Habileté dans un art quelconque.* 1784 *"Pour gagner du bien, le savoir-faire vaut mieux que le savoir."* In order to succeed, savoir faire is more important than knowledge. Pierre Augustin Caron de Beaumarchais, *Le Mariage de Figaro,* V, 3. **5:** To be up to snuff with wit of a thing or two. 1815 "He had great confidence in his *savoir-faire.*" Sir Walter Scott, *Guy Mannering.* **6:** Operating knowledge of business sense and sensibility.

CONTENTS

WOMEN, WORK
& THE ART
of
SAVOIR FAIRE

Speaking to an audience of 2,500 women in a Boston ballroom at what was billed as a premier leadership conference for women in business, I said, "So, here's a question for you: Excluding family members, and not counting peers you go to for routine help, *do you have a senior person in business who consistently offers you sound counsel and support and who champions you?* In short, is there a person you've had or have who is your mentor? Raise your hand if you have someone." Perhaps 15 percent of the women raised their hands. "Okay, new question: Raise your hand if you like chocolate." Easily 80 percent of the women shot up hands. Scientific? No. Telling? Yes. Women may share a lot of things (like a love for chocolate!), but having a strong mentor isn't one of them.

We all need a special someone (or two) we can ask questions of and turn to for help . . . someone we can count on to extend him- or herself for us. I know I do. And I wish I'd had suitably informed people to turn to as my professional life evolved, even people who could speak with me via the printed page. I've written this book partly in response to the remarkable number of women who came up to me after I spoke at a conference or business school or who emailed me from all around the world after reading one or both of my *French Women* books asking me to write just this sort of book, from my life's perspective and in my own style.

As I wrote it, I found myself thinking about the scores of women who have sat across from me in job interviews—those who have worked for me and with me over the years; the people I have worked for (some good, some not so good)—and I thought about the things I wanted to say to them at the time but couldn't because it wasn't quite "appropriate." Now's my chance.

What I can tell you, *chère* reader, is what I wanted to tell all those women over the years, whether it's about how best to present yourself to a future employer, how to balance the demands of "work" and "life," or how to relax and enjoy yourself even when you're feeling the pressure of too many demands and not enough time. A sweeping "women's issue" is achieving a healthy balance of work life with *life* life—certainly an imperative amid the pressures of personal responsibilities and gratifications and the still-emerging class of business challenges, expectations, and pressures. What's the point of being a successful businesswoman if you are not happy and are suffering a messy and unhealthy personal life?

Someone said I should call this book *French Women Don't Get Fired*. The problem, though, is they *do* get fired . . . and I couldn't possibly deliver a fail-safe recipe for holding onto your job. What I have tried to write is the sort of book I wish I had been given when starting out in the working world and had at hand along the way. This isn't another business book that tells you how to "succeed" or "get the corner office." Yes, of course, you'll find advice on getting ahead and getting promoted . . . but more than that, you'll find advice on being happy and living a good life, even while you are making the biggest contribution you can to the workplace. That's why I dare to talk about style and clothes and food and wine and entertaining and LIFE in a business book. We don't work in a vacuum. Our work is part of the rest of our lives.

I want to emphasize that you can work smarter and healthier than a lot of people, and you can reap the benefits. That's one form of *savoir faire*. I remember my first meaningful job in New York in public relations. I had no training or real experience in PR; I was a trained translator-interpreter. I did not think I was qualified for the PR position, but the classified ad in the *New York Times* described what seemed like such a dream job for me that I applied anyway. But so did thirty others. That I got the job was a wonder to me and, like a lot of people starting a new job (really a new stage in life and career), I was a bit scared that I might not be up to the challenge. It turned out that I was, and at my three-month review, I had grown the courage to ask my boss why he had chosen me over all those people with stronger PR experience and backgrounds. "I could not even write a press release," I said, still full of wonder. "Mireille, anyone can learn to write a press release," he answered. "Your general knowledge, enthusiasm, and language skills set you apart from the others." We are who we are, but we can learn new things all the time, evolve over time by working hard and smart, and realize our potential. Plus others (like my clairvoyant PR boss) can see talent and potential in us that sometimes we can't for ourselves.

I learned through my two bestselling *French Women* books that if I share my experiences and highlight some of the lessons I have learned, I can have a helpful influence on people who are eager for a little coaching and wish to join a community of like-minded women. Plus, life experienced, observed, and communicated by a woman to a woman is just not the same as getting it from a male perspective, something many businessmen do not yet realize or are helpless to do anything about. Over the course of my career I went from that PR job to board meetings of multi-billion-dollar companies (and divisions) held in global capitals where at 8:30 a.m., self-possessed executives lit up their cigars—*noblesse oblige*—and hours later the smoke was still rising, though the quality of discourse was not. At one meeting I vividly recall, I caught a division leader firing up his laptop with pornography. Seeing me seeing him, he said, "I need it in the morning to get me going." (You cannot make this stuff up.) Have you noticed that the author of almost any business book, whether self-help, textbook, memoir, or biography, is usually someone who has never been mistaken for a secretary? Not a surprise, since more than 90 percent of CEOs and corporate board members are men.

Now, I confess that I am no professor of business, management consultant (a new term is management therapist), or career guru. I am, however, a seemingly accomplished businesswoman with thirty years of perspective on the practice of business in America and internationally, the evolving role of women in business, and the global transformation of the marketplace. Plus I try to be a pilgrim in addressing the cultural exigencies of modern business and life through a balanced and healthy lifestyle.

I have certainly had a charmed business life—not that I have not been screamed at by drug-addicted megalomaniacs (well, one) or tolerated some awkward colleagues with reptilian IQs yet soaring egos—but I have been at the table during a strikingly transitional period for women in business, and have experienced a meal of small, medium, and large business in private and public versions . . . with even a little government bureaucracy thrown in (hey, I was born French). One characteristic of my career and part of why I wrote this book now, which I hope will help fill a gap in women-centric communications, is that I write from a global perspective with a footprint in three centuries and many countries. Being a French woman (and an American citizen) and having worked for a French company, I believe I wear the kind of cross-cultural glasses that help one see some of the obvious characteristics of our working environment that can be lost on us when we are in the middle of it. We lose perspective. The French Champagne company I joined in 1984 was still a venerable family-controlled enterprise run by a fading generation of aristocrats using nineteenth-century human resource and business practices. Though they were very nice people, their awareness of women in business started and ended with perhaps the first "modern" businesswoman, Madame Clicquot, who was born in 1777 and died in 1866. Overnight I became the highest-ranking woman at Veuve Clicquot since Madame Clicquot. (One of my lasting secret pleasures was when the chairman of the company, a true gentleman with whom I still visit, Count Alain de Vogüé, would absentmindedly call me or refer to me as Madame Clicquot.) Two rapid mergers later, and the Veuve Clicquot group of companies became one of the major components of today's LVMH, the world's largest luxury goods company. That proved to be a business culture change of no small order, and my business world grew up in a hurry, from an initial consortium of successful French companies left with considerable independence to today's LVMH, a twenty-first-century global conglomerate.

In 1975, *Time* magazine declared we were entering the "Year of Women." I'd say they printed that story at least a quarter century too soon. Sure, women like me were maturing then with a new sense of identity and opportunity and entering new fields, but the tangible results were a generation away and not just in the corner offices and boardrooms. At the time less than 10 percent of practicing attorneys and physicians in America were women. Today the numbers are nearer 30 percent and climbing. Women still represent less than 20 percent of the United States Congress. But the real change has been in education, nationally and internationally. For the past two decades in the United States, far more women in the 18–24 age group have attended college than ever before, and women now make up the majority of college students. In developed and developing nations alike, the future belongs to the emerging class of female professionals. In some regions of the world, the Middle East among them, daughters en masse are being afforded the opportunity to attain a higher education for the first time, and a set of careers and career paths important to the global economy are becoming open to women.

The lessons learned for women (and men) during this global transition period in business, government, and governance are timely and appropriate for the twenty-first century. As I have often said, I don't want to live in the past but learn from the past. What's here is, I hope, timely and contemporary for now, right now. This book, with its personal illustrations, is essentially about ideas, not about me—some old ideas, perhaps some new ideas, and certainly some newly packaged ideas. I have tried to cull ideas from decades of life experience and incorporate them into an original ratatouille made for perhaps the very first time with an added special ingredient. I hope you like ratatouille. (If I were a man, by the way, I would have used a sports, not a cooking, metaphor.)

Ideally, the thoughts presented here can stimulate introspection and personal growth no matter where you are along the career road. The ideas are wide-ranging, from style to stress and even to etiquette, reflecting that a life in business is holistic and about pleasures more than pain. This book is not a textbook—you will not learn the five keys to running a better meeting, or the six essentials for dealing with difficult colleagues. It contains strategic ideas, values, experiences, lessons learned, stories, essays, and morsels of advice. This book is about helping women (and a few men, *peut-être*) to grow the knowledge, know-how, and tools for empowerment and balance in today's business world. *Allons-y!*

LIFE IS LIVED IN EPISODES AND STAGES

I n just over two months' time, I was going to start my dream job: translator at the Council of Europe in Strasbourg, France. Then chance or fate intervened.

Six months earlier, my first serious position after college as a translator-interpreter and small-projects manager in the Paris office of a Swedish company had ended abruptly when the office was closed during one of those periodic tough economic times that leads to downsizing. I had worked there more than a year and was given a bit of severance pay. Quite a bonanza for a girl in her twenties. And it got better.

I needed a job, of course, and that led me to set my sights on the Council of Europe, which for young and innocent *moi* was the ultimate employer on my radar screen. I aced the qualifying exam and was offered a position as a translator starting the next session, in the fall. So, in the meantime, I used my severance pay to travel to America and Greece and on the spur of the moment took a last-minute discounted American Express weekend to Istanbul.

On a bus from the airport to the hotel there, a handsome fellow with longish curly hair, blue eyes, and a deep tan said to me in French, *"Vous êtes très intelligente de voyager avec un p'tit sac...."* (You are very smart to travel so light).

I always travel light, but in this case it was because I had left my suitcase back in Athens.

I figured he was Turkish. He wasn't.

He was an American from New York who had seen the same discounted trip from Athens to Istanbul.

He became my companion for the next few days, and then for another few days back in Athens, and then for another few days, and then I was hopelessly in love.

We wanted to continue our relationship, but he had to return to America, where he was completing his Ph.D. I went back to France. For the next weeks I faced what turned out to be the most important decision of my life. A classic: the job, the man, the city, the country?

Familiar with it? The country, the city, the man, the job. The man or the job . . . the job or the man?

Forget all my previous planning and dreaming, I chose the man and New York, my husband and home now for more than thirty years. I never took up my early dream of working at the Council of Europe.

So much for planning, in business or in life. Lesson learned. Things happen. Opportunities are often unpredictable.

Life is lived in episodes and stages. Episodes because they are roughly self-contained and somewhat arbitrary, at least as they relate to time and place. Stages because they evolve out of one another and are linear and in many cases inevitable, like adolescence or one's first professional position. Business, too, is lived in episodes and stages, and it has a sometimes cruel way of disarming our passions and shrugging off some of our most prized abilities as commonplace or irrelevant.

....

PURSUING ONE'S GIFTS

One stage in my life began when I was a teenager in Eastern France and discovered a passion for languages—my native French, increasingly important English, and old-world German, then the preeminent first language in Europe (though no one outside Germany wanted to admit it). When we are good at something—and I was very good at the study of languages— aren't we proud and motivated to pursue it and encouraged to do so by others? Sure. People who are good at music, dance, or athletics, for instance, fill their early years pursuing their gifts and pleasures, perhaps even becoming world-class performers or nearly so, and some even turn professional. But generally not for long.

My interest in language and culture led me to become a high school exchange student outside Boston, then a college student in Paris, and eventually helped bring me to America to be with my soon-to-be husband, Edward, where I worked in the proverbial fields. Early on I was a translator, including for the UN, then, following my passion, I toiled in the lowest of the low positions at the New York office of Food and Wine from France. Then I moved on to a New York PR-advertising firm where I leveraged my French heritage and a bit of knowledge to become a director of the Champagne Bureau, a trade organization and U.S. division of the CIVC (Comité Interprofessionnel du Vin de Champagne), promoting the entire Champagne industry. That's when—college internships and entry-level jobs included—I truly learned business and benefited from the fatherly teachings of the American owner of the agency.

It seemed like a risk to me to take that first professional job in PR. As I've noted, I had no training. I feared I would be unemployed in no time. Even sitting in my own office on Fifth Avenue with a secretary outside my door—Fifth Avenue in New York City!—gave me the willies at first. But then I discovered something about myself and about overcoming fears and anxieties.

Maybe you, like me, can remember walking into your first real job or a new position after a promotion and wondering whether you could live up to your employer's expectations, whatever those were. For me, it turned out that some of my first tasks would involve public speaking and giving radio interviews, activities that rank right up there among people's most common dreads and anxieties. I'd not connected being on the radio with the job before and had never imagined doing it. But my boss explained that I had an opportunity at hand and that handling the media was a responsibility that went with my new position.

Champagne is the traditional drink of New Year's Eve, and a large percentage of annual consumption takes place from late November through January 1. Therefore, those are also the prime weeks for articles and interviews about Champagne. Over the years I have delivered the "how to open a bottle" talk countless times, usually during the last few days of December. Well, the first opportunity I ever had to give that little speech came my way just after I started this new job. I was told that I should pitch to radio stations the opportunity to conduct interviews about Champagne—and then I was to be the one interviewed, mostly live!

Let's say (*entre nous*) I was "anxious" over the charge. I can still remember my hand feeling weak as a I picked up the phone to call the first radio station and pitch them a story about Champagne. I needn't have worried, they wouldn't take my call anyway!

I found dusty old pitch letters in the file. Now, I could have just blown off the cobwebs and sent those out to the same people who had been ignoring them since Prohibition was lifted. But I realized I had an advantage: I had an authentic French accent that people in New York frequently told me they found charming. I needed to have the chance to speak directly with someone who could actually make a decision. Just as a job application letter is designed to get you an interview, the pitch letter needs to be designed to get read and remembered—and by the right person—in order to secure you a spot. (And there are oral versions of pitch letters, too, that need to be polished for use on the phone or in person.) Also, I had to recognize that lots of pitches get tossed out unread (Don't we now do that constantly with emails?). So, first I called to get the name of the current booking manager. That proved to be extremely important. (Never misspell a name or send a letter to someone no longer in a position.) Then I recast the pitch letters to that person, always adding a little distinctive French phrasing at the beginning of the letter. Then the real work began. Knowing in advance that the success rate would not be high, I called and called stations across the country. Then I called some more.

Sometimes people were busy or simply did not want to speak with me (part of the skill set for selling is the ability to accept rejection). Sometimes I got lucky, and people remembered me from the pitch letter. Sometimes I got very lucky and they called me after they got the pitch letter (obviously, in those cases my pitch aligned perfectly with helping them do their job and fill their slots). But mostly I called and called. When I did get through and spoke with a decision maker, including a preliminary one, I enjoyed remarkable success. "Oh, is that a French accent?" That's when I knew I had them and that I had a good voice for radio. We'd talk over the phone about whatever they wanted—from information about their trip to Paris or my recommendations for a French restaurant in New York. As we laughed and built a connection—a key element in successful business—interview after interview got scheduled. And with each interview that took place—from sixty-second spots to sixty-minute programs with call-ins—I not only overcame my fears but discovered that I enjoyed being interviewed and had a talent for it. I learned the importance of doing more than is expected and that there are lots of good ideas in business, but execution is what matters. And you can be most effective when you align your special talents to the task at hand. (What is it that you have your predecessors didn't or your colleagues don't? Perhaps just a better work ethic or simply a distinctive and attractive accent.) Plus there are new approaches to good, old ideas, like the ones I managed to find with the pitch letters. To the astonishment of my boss, I did fifty-three interviews that first season, compared with three the previous one. It was a year's worth of results in a few weeks, and it built my business confidence enormously. And it helped build a stage in my life and career. *C'était le bon temps.*

I could still be doing that today—promoting Champagne across America—what a great job. I progressed quickly to the head of the line to take over the PR firm with its various accounts when the owner retired, but instead I took a chance and moved down one of those roads less traveled, and it made all the difference. So, life and careers are lived in episodes and stages, but taking some calculated chances (read: risks) also makes all the difference. And you cannot always time your opportunities. Controlling one's fears and anxieties by not letting them dictate premature decisions is part of a solid professional skill set. And especially in tough economic times, fear has the tendency to try to pull us by the nose, something that's hard to fight, but being aware of it helps.

....

STARTING OUT WITHOUT *PISTON*

Gaining my career-launching position at the Champagne Bureau in New York was a combination of luck and skill. Certainly it was a case of being in the right place at the right time. But it did not come through any networking or connections. In France and elsewhere, having some "pull" often gets you that first or second job. In French it is called *piston*, and I did not have any . . . something I was painfully aware of when I walked the streets of Paris and then New York searching for a suitable position. No father or uncle, sister or brother to make a call to a colleague for me. In America, meritocracy, college placement offices, and sometimes a mentoring professor-advisor play a larger role than in Europe in helping one get started professionally. Not that networking and some personal pull are not useful, especially as one advances, but in America you can get an interview largely on your own.

In France, it is still much more of a club atmosphere, and I cannot tell you the number of times I've been asked by someone in France to help a friend or colleague's son or daughter, niece or nephew to get a job or internship in New York. I generally do everything I can to help, remembering what it was like to be young and full of dreams as well as confusion and sometimes even hopelessness at that stage in life. I did not always like it when the young aspirant was connected to a top LVMH executive, because then the cultural expectation was that you'd create a position if you did not already have one with his or her name divinely affixed to it, yet that is the way of the world. Still, it is easy to understand parents and relatives who want to do everything they can to help their family members.

I was reminded of how tough it can be to get ahead without a little coaching and *piston* when I met Maria, a European in her late twenties, who was stuck in her entry-level position, living in a faded third-tier European city, and desperate to move to a new stage in life. (Remember that just because you are stuck in a stage now does not mean you cannot move out of it . . . preferably sooner, but it might have to be later.) Her world reminded me of the old European style and customs that I had known but had become distanced from while living in the electricity and culture of New York.

....

MARIA'S NEXT STAGE

Maria is a tall, attractive woman gifted in both science and languages. A top student, she earned a master's degree in biology and took a job at a not-for-profit cancer research center in a small city an hour and a half from where her parents live. And there she stayed in a poorly paid job for two, three, four years, and then into a fifth year. She was more than poised for the next stage in her personal and professional life, but she could not see her way out. Her boss was awful, her work no longer a challenge, and she was chained to her cubicle, so she had little opportunity to explore jobs in another city. Plus, she had no money, less than no money. She had to count on help from her parents, who have modest means, to help her live extremely modestly. Not a pretty picture or rosy future. I am sure many people know or can relate to someone like Maria.

Our paths crossed when she was doing some freelance writing on health and nutrition and I was impressed by her knowl-

....

edge and eventually by her personality, not to mention her ability to communicate in German, English, French, Italian, and Spanish. "I was so bored at work and at nights, I would listen to and sing songs in those languages and read news and articles on the Internet to learn and improve my languages," she explained to me, as if it were nothing.

I met her in person for the first time in New York when a publishing company paid for her to come on the cheap for two days for a job interview. She was incredibly excited by this singular opportunity, but was quickly devastated with disappointment when a visa snafu shot down her dreams.

The episode and her situation moved me, so I told her to be patient and that I'd try to help her. I knew I could do that eventually but did not want to give her false hopes of a magic-wand solution. I invited her to spend some time with us in France, where I got to know her better and probed to find out what she really wanted to do. She started out saying she'd do anything, she was so desperate to get out of her job and city, where being single and young was a signal to get married or move.

Through many discussions of her likes, dislikes, passions and fears, talents, skills, and dreams, we narrowed down the realistic possibilities, starting with the fact that the job should be in Europe, where she could work with proper papers and also not be too far from her family. She likes publishing, but we kept the fields open and focused on positions where she could use her strong presentational and organizational skills to represent a company in management—coordinating a project or running a small department—or perhaps in marketing and public relations.

We polished her résumé, which, because she'd had only one job, greatly underreported her skills, accomplishments, and what she could bring to an employer. We did an inventory of what she could take to a new company or field—from languages and communications skills to math, science, computer skills, and more—all things she had plenty of evidence to support. We reorganized her résumé with added sections to highlight her transferable skills and experiences with concrete data for what she had to offer rather than just what she had done in the past in terms of schooling and job description. In short, we aligned her résumé to show she was qualified for a much higher and broader position than the one she was holding. It was the truth.

I told her it could take a year to find something worth accepting and to be patient. She had a little luxury of time; she wasn't yet thirty. (Try telling that to someone aching to move on in life.) I introduced her to a few people and sent her résumé to a half dozen others. She landed an interview with a Paris-based company, a global hospitality group that needed someone to join their PR and marketing team. (At her nonprofit foundation, she had written newsletters and helped schedule research conferences, so she had relevant, transferable experience . . . plus all those languages.) Perfect. That's when I appreciated that I had to see her through this entire process, and reminded myself that mentoring isn't only opening doors, it is also reaching back and pulling people through them.

Maria was scared and felt unprepared but of course excited for the interview, which kept getting moved between Paris and the Riviera to fit the schedule of the woman who was doing the hiring. The false starts certainly were tough emotionally on Maria. By phone and email from New York, I rehearsed her for the interview. She had very little interview experience, after all. I gave her a mock interview. We teased out the likely questions and rehearsed her answers. What are your strengths? Your weaknesses? What do you bring to this particular job? What interests you about this company and position? Are you willing to work long hours? Travel? Relocate? How is your previous experience relevant? The toughest proved what salary would be acceptable. Maria was ready to take almost anything offered, but I managed to convince her that anything less than twice what she was currently making would be insufficient to move to Paris and live independently though not lavishly. "Wait for the right job, Maria, you still have your old one," I droned on.

"How do I handle the salary question?" she wanted to know. "There are at least three options," I answered. "You can tell her what you are earning now and say nicely that you would not consider a move without an increase. You can tell her what you assume the position pays, thereby getting a number on the table. But I would not do either. In your case, regardless of how the question is posed, I would tell her the salary range that would enable you to move to and work from Paris. Don't waste her time or yours."

A good researcher, she had already surfed the web effectively for all the latest information on the group and was prepared to ask a few informed questions of her own when the opportunity arose in the interview or when she was asked.

Always anticipate being asked if you have any questions . . . and have some good ones ready. Before she set off for the interview, I gave her one more dose of advice I have often shared. When you are sitting in the interviewee's chair, just relax and be yourself. You are who you are, and the safest thing is to show sides of your "regular" self. The person you are speaking with is doing you a favor. They are more qualified than you to know whether the person you present would fit well in their organization. If they choose you, congratulations, you not only win the job but their commitment to helping you succeed in the new position. That's in the interests of both of you.

The interview went well. The woman said she would get back to her about the position, which would not begin for another six weeks. She never did get back to her. (*Typiquement français!*) Another emotional setback and another occasion when Maria needed someone with whom to talk through the situation. I give Maria a lot of credit for taking my advice to heart and not being defensive about needing help. It is important to be able to reach out for help when you need it.

A month or so later, another interview at another company where I had given her an initial contact materialized. This was for a better position, with clear further growth potential, and for a better company—a midsize, multinational family business with a name everyone knows. The woman she would be reporting to travels a lot in Europe and America, and it took a while to fix an interview, which turned out also to be in the South of France. (Hey, it was late summer and perhaps people were looking for excuses to go there.) Maria researched the corporation in preparation for the interview, and I counseled her that this position should pay three or four times what she was earning. "Don't think of taking this for anything less than three times," I said. "They won't respect you if you are willing to accept a cut-rate salary, and this company can easily afford to pay the going rate and more. Plus, you are a highly presentable woman with a master's degree, five years of business experience, and are fluent in five languages." I think from her perspective the money was so much and she was so lacking in opportunities and confidence, she thought I was from a different universe. She needed to show confidence and not succumb to fear or negative thoughts. Being the person to pep her up and advise her was what I had signed on to do, and I was determined that she not sell herself short.

After a good first interview, two HR guys from the corporate office wanted to meet her in Madrid. That interview almost lost her the job for being overqualified, we learned later. I think they must have been intimidated by her education and intelligence. But they said they'd get back to her in a week. They did, and said they'd like her to meet someone else, a top person in Geneva. It seemed at this point they were considering adopting her into the family and the *patron* wanted to meet her, but he would not be available for a couple of weeks. By now, Maria's head was spinning with possibilities and responsibilities. She was thinking about how to resign from her current position—"not till you have something in writing from the new employer," I counseled—when and how to tell her landlord she'd be moving, et cetera, et cetera.

To bring this story to a close, she went to Geneva, got the job, screamed with joy, and was soon on a plane to the United States for a month's training. The job in administration with plenty of hands-on important responsibilities (accompanied by an impressive salary) was so beyond what she was thinking just months earlier, she could hardly believe it was true. "They are sending a car to the airport to meet me and take me to an apartment they rented for me for the month," she told me via Internet phone from the airport on the way to America. It was such a fantasy, only her ecstatic mother, father, and grandmother knew about it. I suspect she was waiting for it to be her "real life" before telling her friends and relatives—for it to move from being an episode to a stage in life. Over the course of a few months and from a bleak situation, a dream became concrete. Life can be like that. It only takes some luck, some talent, some work, and perhaps a little help.

. . . .

MY NEXT STAGE(S)

Yes, but with talent, hard work, and being in the right place you can help make your own luck. By my late twenties I had something of a vision of myself in some sort of management position that permitted me to eat at all the top restaurants on someone else's dollar. C'est vrai. Thanks to my PR position at the Champagne Bureau, I had partly achieved my goal, and through my position I eventually met the heads of all the major Champagne houses (brands) imported to the United States, and at some point

. . . .

most tried to recruit me—therein is a lesson in both networking and patience.

When my "ultimate" came calling, the House of Veuve Clicquot (my mother's favorite Champagne), I was ready. The opportunity to work for Clicquot based in New York promised me work in my chosen field, trips to my native France with the chance to see my parents, and, yes, hundreds of meals in top restaurants every year. So, I enlisted, against a lot of industry advice to the contrary—the strategy would not work, the brand was too far behind in America, the business model was not affordable (all from people who later ate their words in overdoses). I took the leap and became Veuve Clicquot's first employee in a start-up venture in America. In retrospect, I wonder whether these men who were so free with their opinions and predictions were jealous, simply lacking vision, or arrogant in their confidence that if they could not make it work for their brand, I as a less seasoned woman would have no chance of success with Veuve Clicquot. Several of them subsequently lost their brands and went out of business. Yet Clicquot, Inc., the U.S. division of the company, grew into an import and marketing company with a couple of dozen brands from around the world, a top image and reputation, and quite handsome profits, profit margins, and financial turnover (plus eventually more employees and lives to worry about than is fun).

So, again, the lesson learned: Don't let fear be a barrier to your achieving your ambitions. Success, like failure, is relative, and out of a stage of modest professional achievements (failure is such a dramatic and generally inappropriate word), there is always the potential for upside. You can wake up one morning and find that your prospects and perspective have changed overnight. Sometimes it is simply that you are ready to enter a new stage in life and embrace new opportunities and challenges. You then need to go looking for opportunity. Or perhaps an opportunity comes to you and announces, "It's time."

Not that I did not have apprehensions when I decided to make my career move, but I made a calculated decision. I saw how the company and brand could work—such quality, history, and competitive advantages waiting to be exploited—while others did not grasp them, and I embraced the challenge and responsibility to see that it did. Sure, I feared all the things that could go wrong, but if truth be told, the lure of a good challenge and the enticement of perks and a good salary can be the emollients that soothe fears and tip a decision. More important, in this case I could accept the personal risks involved, in part because I had some control over the outcome. Too often we become paralyzed by worry over the worst things that can happen. We lack confidence and security, panic over financial risk, get locked into careers and lifestyles that are not what we dreamed for ourselves or can achieve. Our passions get displaced and we become sad and even depressed. All because we were afraid to take a risk at a moment of opportunity.

Of course, there are risks that prove too risky, and not taking those are some of our best decisions, but those decisions shouldn't be made because of fear but intelligence. The best decisions I made in terms of my personal and professional life were risky ones . . . from moving to America for the man, to (on a more modest level) doing the radio interviews, to signing on to a less-than-certain start-up, where I would stay (and thrive!) for more than two decades, including a long stint as CEO.

Women tend to be caregivers more than men and thus often have some of their "stages" and "episodes" circumscribed by marriage and stages in their husbands' careers, by rearing children, and even caring for older parents. (Until her recent passing, we looked after my ninety-six-year-old mother and are currently still caring for Edward's ninety-three-year-old mother.) Concluding such stages in life presents opportunities and invitations to relaunch or reinvigorate a career or professional life. They are also times when you can make your own luck or at least put yourself in a position to be receptive to "lucky breaks." So, again, think opportunity. Whether these are sad or happy times emotionally, remember not to think failure. (Where does that get you, anyway?)

I did not have a goal or grand strategy for achieving success in business beyond being committed to working harder and smarter (and, I hoped, eating better) than my colleagues and competitors.

In writing about exceptional achievers in *Outliers* (none of them women!), Malcolm Gladwell shares as one of his big ideas that men of genius possess as common traits hard work; stick-to-itiveness when faced with tough challenges and seeming failure; and some good, shrewd people skills. Moreover, he finds their highly successful careers were advanced by lucky breaks, sometimes multiple ones, surprising and unpredictable moments of opportunity and circumstance that these men had the cleverness to capitalize on. Well, that's not true just for men of genius. It works much the same for women of ability, a wide range of ability. And to me, it is about being open and prepared to seize opportunities for a new stage in business and life and to work harder and smarter than the next guy.

CHOOSING A PATH:
PASSION, TALENT, AND MORE

I t is almost a cliché to say that by choosing something you love for a career "you'll never have to work another day in your life." If only it were true. It is not. Unless you just love filling out expense reports and deleting emails and reports that never should have come to you in the first place, you, like me, have spent a good chunk of your work life doing things that you don't like, let alone love. For me it wasn't all drinking Champagne and being pampered at five-star hotels. There is a lot of perspiration that goes into any position along any career path. If you are passionate about your field and what you are doing, though, the good times are great.

You even look better when you are full of passion for what you are doing. Or, as Yves Saint Laurent said, "The most beautiful makeup on a woman is passion, but cosmetics are easier to buy."

As I have told you, I believe that life is lived in episodes and stages, and it is clear that some passions can fade while new ones emerge over time. Indeed, our first loves and passions can be overrated and it would be unwise to pursue them. Others are pursued earnestly for a time, then discarded. *C'est la vie.*

....

BALANCING PASSION WITH OPPORTUNITY

Here's the story of Emily, someone I first met fifteen years ago and recently reconnected with. Emily dreamed of becoming an architect, became one, and moved from her home in the Midwest to New York City to make a career and exploit her passion. Architecture is, of course, a challenging, inspiring, competitive field, and she was toiling away just above the subsistence level when one day at a party she met a woman, her contemporary, who worked for a national magazine. After some pleasant get-to-know-one-another conversation, her new acquaintance said, "Since you're an architect, would you like to write a short review for us of the new Hotel X?" Emily, as you can imagine, said, "I'd love to!" And with that, she began a new stage in her life and career. Her review was well received. She enjoyed applying her "eye" and knowledge in a new way. The first review was followed by several others, and she found she so much enjoyed "the architecture of writing," she applied for and got a full-time position at a magazine as an interiors and design assistant editor (and

....

later editor). I am sure the steady paycheck was nice, but more than that she was completely energized and enthralled by traveling to beautiful homes or new buildings, writing articles, supervising photography, seeing the country, staying at top hotels.

I learned that after a few years and after she started to raise a family, she left to become a freelance writer to better balance her time, responsibilities, and priorities. She also used that period and her architectural training to renovate a "fixer-upper" home. When I reconnected with her, she was happily back full time as a magazine editor, doing a good deal of writing, and no longer thought of herself as an architect but rather as a discerning wordsmith, critic, and editor.

Emily's story (and I know several women with similar detours and tales) demonstrates that our passions (such as architecture) can be honored in unexpected ways—we need to be open to channeling them into good and rewarding opportunities.

Chance opportunities and new passions don't strike only women starting their careers; they can occur anytime. I knew a woman in her late twenties who went from working in banking to being the founder and co-owner of what became a successful children's clothing business. She loved the change and challenge (and the kids). I also have a long-standing friend "*d'un certain âge*," as we say in France, whose husband ran a successful and reasonably large family tool and die business while she tended to their six children. When he suddenly died in his forties, she decided to take over as CEO, in part to serve her family. So this was a sort of arranged business marriage born out of necessity. She'd been on the board and knew the business from the dinner table, but she was not (in this case literally) a nuts-and-bolts person. But she is a doer, a natural leader, the outgoing life of a party, and she found out she *loved* business. She loved the challenges, the people, the networking, the sales and rewards. Under her leadership, the company grew and grew, and she was one of the happiest and most balanced business leaders I met over the years. And today, with her sons running the corporation, she is one of the happiest retired business leaders I know. She is the first to tell you how much the business gave to her and how she discovered passions and abilities she never knew she had.

....

"YOU GOTTA HAVE HEART"

Life is not a rehearsal, so whatever you choose to do, it is good if your heart is in it. I thought of this when I came across the story of George Lillie Craik, who in the mid-1860s became a partner in the venerable publishing house of Macmillan & Co. For the next forty years, when he passed staff members at their desks he would ask them, "Is your heart in your work?" And for another forty years, his spirit, words, and legend lived on among the aging employees who remembered him fondly.

Craik had integrity, energy, and passion for what he did. He asked a seemingly simple question: Is your heart in your work? That's a good thing to ask ourselves. It helps us to get up early on Monday morning and to stay late on Thursday night to do things right. And if your heart is no longer in your work, what is

....

that telling you? Is it faded passion or a poor work situation? Is it time to move on and/or change career?

A key factor for me is being comfortable with and even proud of the field, company, and position where I work. We can't all be sports announcers or movie directors or whatever is popular these days with college freshmen. I felt good about working in the Champagne and wine business. I gave a lot of people pleasure with some of life's affordable luxuries, and I don't think I hurt anyone. Perhaps I would have felt better and nobler being a nurse or a Peace Corps worker, but that just isn't me, I suspect, and the opportunities never materialized for me to become one of those things.

There's the question, though, of believing that you know where your heart lies and then finding out if in reality you are correct. At any stage in life, people, I find, are pretty clear on a few things they are really passionate about, vocationally and avocationally, so exploring career options is really an exercise in getting a bit granular. Who knew you could get paid for catching butterflies? Being a translator-interpreter was sublimely appealing to nineteen-year-old me. Studying five years to become one was enjoyable. Then came the job. About a year of that and I knew I had chosen the wrong field. I was not being asked to meet the challenges of translating literary masterpieces. In the business and government sectors where I worked, it was too much translating of either meaningless make-nice boilerplate or highly technical contracts or scientific documents for people who increasingly knew English (I translated from English into French) and would probably not read what I was laboring to get right, anyway. Actually, the field had not changed, but my understanding of it had.

....

BALANCING TALENT WITH PASSION
WITH OPPORTUNITY

Too much talent can be a burden—you may be driven to exploit it, with everyone encouraging you and giving you so much positive reinforcement that you get pushed in a direction convinced that you like it. A lot of little girls spend hours ice-skating or doing gymnastics or playing the flute (am I stereotyping? Add math equations, science research, and basketball), encouraged because they are the best in their little town or county. How many kids (and their doting parents) think based on a fourth-grade talent show that Hollywood is waiting? And if you are the best in your region, you may well become consumed with your serious talent at the expense of other sides of your personality and other talents. It can become something of a vicious circle; the more you devote to your standout talent, the better you get at its application and the less time and development you apportion to other areas.

Eventually you have a reality check. Just because you edited the high school newspaper doesn't mean you have the talent to be a correspondent for *60 Minutes* or a reporter for the *New York Times*. While in my heart I admire and embrace, say, musicians, my head steps in at times and says engineering is a much better career path, especially for a woman. And regardless of how creative or ambitious the work is, even the most seemingly desirable careers have downsides. If you have the right math and science gene, could you become passionate about and successful at some sort of science career in areas where historically women rarely tread? I am, of course, raising the debate we all must go through of talent versus opportunity versus passion. We know there are growth fields and advancement opportunities and the reverse. Well, there is passion as in irresistible lust and there is passion as in intimacy and trust. Consider, if you will, the arranged marriage.

The idea of having one's parents pick one's life partner is still commonplace in some societies and cultures today. In other societies and cultures, where there is the belief that courtship, compatibility, and sexual appeal must kick off a union, the idea of an arranged marriage is shocking. Obviously, most parents who arrange marriage for their children want the marriages to succeed, and these parents believe they have the wisdom from experience to know what to look for in partners. Defining a "successful" marriage can include a number of debatable criteria, but studies show that arranged marriages are often as, if not more, successful than love matches, and that partners who meet for the first time at the altar often develop true love and passion for one another that sustains them through life. And the point as related to careers? One's first love and passion can be overrated and unwise to pursue. A passion for what you do helps you get up in the morning, and you should work in a field that you enjoy; however, you can develop a healthy love for fields you never considered or in some cases never heard of or encountered before, or in fact may not ever have existed before. Your heart should be in your work, but that doesn't mean your work has to be something you have *always* loved.

The enlightened career move has to balance talent with passion and opportunity. Nature did not give us the bodies to succeed in certain professions or the minds for others. There is nothing like doing a personal SWOT analysis (identifying strengths, weaknesses, opportunities, and threats) to position you for the future.

When I became disillusioned with languages as a career despite my once-consuming passion and gift for them, I had to figure out what I wanted to do when I grew up (I had a few years before I reached thirty). I fretted over and was confused by all the possibilities. After a decade of having a clear direction, I was anxious because I did not have one. I worked and reworked my personal SWOT analysis, though I didn't know what it was called. Then one day Edward said, "Well, it is obvious to anyone who knows you, you're passionate about food, wine, and travel." True, but until then the little light that said I could have a career in these areas had not gone off in my head. It may have been obvious to everyone . . . but not to me. That helped trigger more introspection, and I added comparative cultures and then lifestyles, especially healthy lifestyles, to my inventory of likes, interests, and passions. And then, once "I knew myself," I was able to balance passion and talent with opportunity toward a career choice and path. Of course, I had to sort out the viable options from the fantasies, but soon I answered that classified ad that led to everything else. I have a bit of charisma, with a French accent and a personal style, and I happened to end up in the wine and spirits industry, where all it takes is reasonable intelligence to be successful, plus some specialized abilities, including those related to sales and marketing, that don't appear on standardized tests.

It is a lot easier if you put in the time brainstorming and investigating your career choices rather than taking years in living out episodes and stages that you will discard later because they led to the wrong fields and positions. Easier said than done, *bien sûr*, but some of it comes naturally as we evolve as a person—call it experience and maturity—and help can come from friends and mentors who can sometimes see us more clearly than we can see ourselves. Don't be afraid to ask for advice. College advisors, for example, can spot talents and point out careers, and later spouses and partners or even HR counselors can help point out where your heart and talent meet.

Food, wine, travel, and associated cultures led to my career rather than other things that I might have done in large part through a process of elimination. I was much clearer about what I did not want to do or could not do than what things I could and would do. So, when I wiped away a huge swath of careers and fields in a deductive process, I felt relieved and had a manageable group of potential jobs that I further reduced by aligning opportunities (as in realistic job openings and avenues) with my talents and passions. I can also tell you that I came to enjoy some of the things (both big and little) that I did not at first envision myself doing, such as reading the *Wall Street Journal* weekday mornings, and now on Saturdays as well (especially since they added the personal journal section). And what that says, again, is that when you find a

field that is a comfortable fit for you, you will grow within it and
you will come to enjoy and perhaps love some of the things that
you did not know existed or thought you would not like.

....

A CASE IN POINT

We started Clicquot, Inc., the American subsidiary of Veuve
Clicquot Ponsardin, with me as vice president for communications and marketing (a story in itself, as the word *marketing* did
not exist in France or in French, and the concept was barely understood by the venerable board of Veuve Clicquot). But marketing was by then my métier, and I was accepted immediately as
the authority on the subject and came to have a shaping global
influence. On paper, the president was the export director in
France. A nice, sharp person, but thousands of miles and many
time zones away, in an era before email. So, apart from periodic
meetings and faxes and phone calls to France, Australia, Italy, or
wherever he was, I minded the U.S. business. We also recruited
and then again recruited a vice president for sales as the other key
person in the management team. I handled getting people to buy
VCP (Veuve Clicquot Ponsardin); he was supposed to get the
bottles into the places where people could buy them. I worked
almost exclusively with men both in France and across America
at old-line distributors better known for hard liquor sales (and
profits) than for selling wine, and I encountered many a former
liquor salesmen at a time when America was just awakening to
wine at the table.

....

Partly because I was French with a French-American/American-French perspective, a good communicator, and so earnest and passionate, my colleagues back in France began to trust my judgment more and more, and I wound up doing more and more—from shopping for office leases (I went with the CFO and was mistaken for his secretary) to recruiting and dismissing distributors.

I had a mini-epiphany after we let our third VP of sales go in the early years of our company, even as our sales and reputation grew (you know the story about low-hanging fruit—there was plenty to pick when we started). I recognized that if I took responsibility for that job myself, it would be easier than sitting politely at meetings listening to what I knew were less than scintillating ideas, or being embarrassed in public by others' actions, or doing others' work for them. Profound, *oui?* Seems obvious now, but at the time, it was a seismic shift in my thinking (and confidence). So, with a few years under my belt (even though I mostly did not wear a belt), I was ready, and said to my boss back in France, okay, I'll give it a try as president and CEO.

To quiet my apprehensions now that I was in charge of marketing *and* sales *and* finance *and* operations, I quickly set about taking a few one- or two-day seminars geared to helping me do my job better in finance, human resource management, and other areas, as well as talking to friends and reading more business books and periodicals. Throughout my career, I kept up with the practice of signing up for a couple of seminars or conferences a year designed to help me work better (and not the gimmicky kind that prepares you in seven easy steps to be a VP, CEO, or ruler of the universe) as part of my personal development program. I recommend it.

With each challenge and each success my passion for the job grew. With me as president and CEO—*merci beaucoup*—we continued to grow and hire the best talent available and follow the best business practices (not always getting either right the first time), but I was the one counted on to lead the firm and handle everything from negotiating contracts to hiring and firing staff (not my idea of fun), to mergers and acquisitions (I led the search for and eventually purchased a Napa Valley winery, and ran, then "de-accessed," another California winery), to being acquired (by LVMH as part of a merger), to working with lawyers and more lawyers and accountants and suppliers (hey, I already said it wasn't all drinking Champagne in posh locations), to marketing campaigns to strategic plan after strategic plan (five-year, one-year, annual revision 1, 2, and 3) and financial report after financial report (daily, weekly, monthly, quarterly, annually . . .), from serving on small boards to billion-dollar boards and international committees, et cetera, et cetera. And meetings? I never cared much for meetings, and as CEO I had to attend and often run far too many, often traveling to states and countries (especially France) for ten minutes of useful information and face-to-face exchanges. All part of the job. And it's so helpful if you are passionate about the core business and field.

The high-end wine and spirits industry and the top echelon of the luxury goods sectors where I spent my business career were not, are not populated by Phi Beta Kappa graduates. Over the years, though, I met some really smart people, especially owners of American wineries. There's a joke in the business: "How do you make a small fortune in the wine business?" "Start with a large one." And that's what a lot of people have done (not that they really lost their mining, industrial, banking, or whatever fortunes they had built, they just poured them endlessly into the ground—as in vineyards, vines, equipment, and more). They were smart and successful in another field and then bought themselves a winery following a late-maturing passion. Generally speaking, I met warm, generous, and capable people in the wine and luxury sector.

I don't mean to sound arrogant, but I know without a doubt that my company's business success was achieved by my team's working smarter than the competition. I don't believe I would have been nearly as successful in a host of other sectors, from academia to finance to medicine. What I did find was, for me, the perfect triad of talent, passion, and opportunity. I did not know I'd found it at first, but as soon as I recognized it, I dropped anchor.

THE PRINCIPLE OF
ENLIGHTENED SELF-INTEREST

Growing up in a small town in Eastern France, with parents who were small business owners, I had little or no exposure to the corporate world. There was a dying factory in our town, so I eventually learned about early retirements and severance packages and how people depend on the government for a security blanket. But corporate politics, practices, cultures, cruelties, leaders, role models? Not a lick. Nor was it something that graced the papers, TV shows, or the schools during my formative years. Where I learned was on the job.

Today, everyone knows or should know that employers buy your time and rent your mind but don't own it or you. I can state that without rancor; it is just the way it is. You know that, they know that, but it goes unspoken, of course, and sometimes in the midst of things it goes unremembered by you or them. Did I state that too strongly? Some employers are good, lots are not, and at points along the routine continuum of a career with all its exigencies, your self-interests will come to be at odds with your supervisor's or your company's. Those are personal decision-making occasions, and over the years when faced with such challenges, I learned to say to myself: *Act with enlightened self-interest.*

It is a principle I have used often and it figures elsewhere in this book, but what is it? First, let me tell you what it is *not*. It is not acting selfishly. Selfish behavior doesn't get you very far very often. It is easily spotted and universally not respected, especially in a leader or colleague.

To act with enlightened self-interest you have "to know thyself," and step out of your immediate body full of instant passions, including anger, love, jealousy, and perhaps even hate. (The failure to know oneself is, of course, at the core of all classic Greek tragedies.) You need to make a cold analysis of your situation in context. You need, for instance, to see, understand, and weigh your company's plans and interests alongside your own unit's or supervisor's and then see yourself as a third and more vital unit. Then run the behavioral options for all three—the what-ifs from multiple perspectives. Often, what you want to do in your gut is, upon reflection, not in your true best interest. (So much self-help guidance is based on the notion of following one's heart, but, again, reality is usually more complicated than that.) It is almost always in your enlightened self-interest to make your boss look good and not find excuses for your actions or attitudes or lack of credit due. (This is sometimes called "upward management," understanding and fulfilling your boss's and perhaps your boss's boss's needs; I see it as basic business sense.) But how many get and remember that lesson? Also recognize that the higher up the totem you climb, it is the company performance, not individual performance, that is viewed and counts most. At any level, we are all cogs in a bigger wheel (unless you own the company and have a rubber-stamp board . . . if so, enjoy!).

....

CHANGEZ DE PLACE

Acting in enlightened self-interest comes up often in terms of career moves, as in promotions or job changes. In one sense, enlightened self-interest is creating your own luck and opportunities and making the most of them. Today a lot of people switch companies and jobs several times on their way to wherever they think they want to get. I remember interviewing a young woman who tried to explain to me why she had had eight jobs in twelve years. Her explanation was that she often learned what she needed to know at each one after six months. While there's something to be said for confidence and aggressiveness in the practice of business, this woman's response was *not* enlightened (and could be taken as intellectual arrogance and immaturity). She certainly was not considering her audience. We weren't looking to hire someone and invest in them for a return tenure of a year. And a word of advice, don't go into an interview without good answers to the predictable tough questions.

....

Someone like her could have acted with enlightened self-interest in building her career by saying to herself, "I've got this red flag on my résumé, suggesting among a long list of things that I won't stay long at a new job, or perhaps I burn bridges and my ex-employers are not sorry to see me go, or that I am confused and don't know what I want to do." Then she could have done something about it, like resolve to stick with her job another six months or another year, even though she may have believed she was ready for a new challenge, disliked her boss, and had learned everything she needed to know. At the minimum she should tell herself, "I am not going to quit in November or December. I am going to wait another month or two and grab another digit." By doing so, a seemingly one-year stint, say, September 2008 to November 2009—could, by ending in February 2010 legitimately appear on her résumé as 2008–2010 and convey a bit more consistency and stability.

An "enlightened" argument for changing positions and companies once or twice is that one gains new skills by performing a different function and experiencing different business cultures and management styles. That argument sells in an interview and in life. On the way up the ladder, exposure to different business areas can be part of your talent development, rather like taking different classes at school. You can broaden your experience, for instance, by taking a lateral position for at least a year (if you can) in, say, marketing if you are currently working in finance. Or volunteer for extra work in another department for a month or more when that department is temporarily short-staffed. It's not always possible, but you've got nothing to lose by asking;

you'd signal your interest in becoming more well rounded, and sooner or later you might be given a little project in another area or be added to an interdisciplinary team. Cross-pollination is a good thing. Actually having worked on a reconciliation project or an event plan and being able to talk about it is more substantive than attending periodic professional seminars or in-house workshops, which are great booster shots for doing your job better but are not highlights on a résumé, nor do they groom one all that well for promotion. There's no substitute for sustained hands-on experience. And concrete exposure to a variety of business functions is one of the solutions to how do you get to the next upward position. My work in national sales certainly helped me better lead Clicquot, Inc. And while marketing was once a key feeder to the C-suite, today it has been overtaken by experience in finance.

I once had a sales manager, a very good sales manager, who after perhaps eight years and a couple of promotions, started asking to attend communications and marketing meetings, and then to work partly in that department, and then to pick up a leadership role in that area. By acting in enlightened self-interest, along the way he did pick up some solid experience in marketing. In a tough job market (when isn't it?), he positioned himself to seize an opportunity for advancement in sales, marketing, or administration. Today he is the vice president of marketing for a major wine importer.

When building a career, it is almost always in one's enlightened self-interest to leave on good terms with one's employer and supervisor. That is not always easy or possible, but it is good for you when it happens. There's certainly no fail-safe course of action when you are looking for a new job while holding another job. If you are lucky enough to have a mentor (who is not your boss), that's a good person to consult. Every situation is unique because of the personalities and history involved. If you've been passed over for a promotion or have been in the same position for a long time because the next promotion would be your supervisor's position, and s/he is not going anywhere soon to the best of your knowledge, then your conscience should be clear as you quietly pursue your next position. (I am speaking these days with a mid-career woman, a casual acquaintance, who reached out to me because she has been working insane hours and has been stuck in the same mid-management position year after year. What to do? She likes the field and the work, but is it she, her boss, the corporate culture, or the economy that keeps her spinning in place with "proper" salary increases and no more? Should she move on or stick it out? We don't know yet . . .) If you are locked in place, the fact that you are looking either casually or aggressively for a new job would come as no surprise to your supervisor or coworkers who would respect your actions. I always had a sense when people were getting ready to leave and generally was aware of their reasons for doing so.

It is often a risky, disquieting period when you are actively pursuing a new position, and especially when you are a finalist for one. What if your boss finds out? Small chance they will hear directly; more likely that a colleague will find out and tell your boss out of loyalty to her and the company. To tell or not tell your supervisor that you are looking? No question, it is easier not to tell. It is a passive action. Telling takes some courage and carries a lot of risk. You could be gone tomorrow. For the record, most people don't tell. It should be noted that being up front has some upside potential, from possibly gaining some respect to getting a raise or promotion without having challenged your supervisor to top an offer in hand.

In any case, once you have made a firm decision to leave your position and are not just testing the waters or exploring a "feeler," you've crossed the Rubicon and are in a position to speak with your supervisor without much risk. Once committed, in most cases saying you are going sooner rather than later and at a point before s/he would find out for herself is probably best . . . at least if you care about leaving on good terms and hope to stay in touch at some point down the road. And let me tell you, it is remarkable how people have a way of resurfacing in your life years and years after you seemingly have departed from them or lost touch. Giving just two weeks' notice without a morsel of flexibility can burn bridges.

The timing of your departure(s) is often the key to exiting with your former company's goodwill. If you are doing a good and valuable job, your supervisor and company won't be happy about your leaving anytime (it is in their interests for you to stay and stay in the box you are in perhaps forever), but if you are leaving for a truly better opportunity, and if you time your search and departure at a relatively good time in the business cycle for them—say, when a big project is coming to an end, your tasks are neatly packaged, or when the key selling season is under control, you can leave with their understanding and respect.

The assumption underlying this advice is that you are working for a reasonably good company with reasonably good management. If you are not, get out at the earliest opportunity. That's also acting in enlightened self-interest. If you are not being treated well as a person—if you truly are being treated with disrespect—don't worry about leaving on good terms (probably not possible in this situation, anyway) or about the consequences of leaving. Just move on.

Understand that whatever your role, from the company's perspective, seen from several cloud layers above your flying level, you are not a person; you are a box and function on an organizational chart. Sad but true. (Am I again stating it too strongly?) Your needs as a person rarely figure in corporate decision making, even at small companies. And even if you are friends outside work with some key decision makers, or at least think you are friends (it is a common mistake to think that colleagues you get along with are really friends when it is only the circumstances of your employment that create a bond), when tough decisions are being made, they will make business decisions in the best interest of the company. It's not personal, it's business, as the saying goes. That's why reorganizations are tough on some people. Your box on the chart can get swept away or modified in a way so that you no longer fit in. You can understand this reality and use it to your advantage or choose to be bitter and jaded.

I've lived through strategic realignments from a number of angles and positions. I've been personally affected, and once I had to dismiss an entire sales force without ever meeting them, from a company we acquired. So, they were literally boxes on a piece of paper. I did meet their general manager, and my company did the right thing by these people. As a woman did I handle this differently than if I were a man? I would like to think so, but probably not. In these situations, the degrees of legal, personal, and practical freedom possible for variation from the established text are limited. Over the years I continued to interact cordially with that sales manager, who more than landed on his feet; indeed, he is now president of a major spirits house. A reminder that treating people professionally and well is always a good rule—you never know, but you can count on some of them remaining in or returning to your professional life in unexpected ways.

So, treating everyone professionally and well is a way of acting in enlightened self-interest. Remember, you are being paid to represent your company well and to do your job effectively. I certainly did not like everyone I entertained or did business with across a desk or conference table, but relatively few, I suspect, could ever read my true feelings. They always knew quite clearly what I thought about their ideas, but not about their persons. And if you ever see yourself in play on an org chart, remember to step outside your emotions and act with enlightened self-interest.

....

LEARN TO SAY NO

Nothing invites you to learn to say no more than a new job offer or promotion. One of the biggest career decisions I ever made was to turn down a promotion . . . twice. I was asked to return to

....

France to run Veuve Clicquot's global operations as CEO. I gave it a lot of thought. I did the usual listing of pros and cons, but in the end, it was not the position best suited to my interests or talents. I knew I could do the job, but I could not see myself, among other things, spending a lot of time in Reims, France. I prefer New York and Paris, and that is a self-interested decision. I had little interest in negotiating with labor unions (whom I respect) or entertaining the farmers who grow the grapes (which I have done) or, worst of all, dealing with all the French system's procedural garbage as a regular responsibility. All those are valuable and necessary (well, perhaps not all the procedural and administrative paperwork), but they're outside my natural inclinations and strongest abilities. Some years later, when the idea was floated again, I was able to pass respectfully, without investing any time or psychic energy.

If you are good at your job, somewhere along the road you will get unsolicited job offers. Some are mighty tempting, and the grass will often look greener over there. That's when the ability to say no becomes an acquired talent. I once turned down an increasingly tempting offer (that is, they kept raising the remuneration to get my attention) to run a large multinational drinks company. Again, it meant leaving New York, and I wasn't in love with the brands in the portfolio (they may have been world-class, but I confess, I'm spoiled), and knowing the hard and hardly glamorous work involved—heavy lifting for a few years at least—I just could not see myself being happy, so I declined. For a number of years, subsequent developments suggested I had made a poor financial decision. So it goes. Looking back, though, things worked out well, and it was another excellent experience in using the word "no." No regrets, just the opposite.

Learning to say no is hardly restricted to job opportunities. I said no to having children. I said no to relocating. I said no to a host of lifestyle temptations and jobs. There are always other jobs, and what's the point of regrets over unknowns or even knowns? It is human to play "what if," but not a particularly valuable use of time, except to take away sound lessons for a better future. Life's too short to worry about the past. And after a while, believe me, you can't even remember the details of the past that were once so consuming. Move on. We all have made mistakes or think we have; living is about the moment and the future. Look ahead.

The most important veto we can exercise is over demands on our time. You know the adage: If you want something done ask a busy person to do it. It's one way to earn points, but after a while too many yeses can destroy you. If you don't maintain a healthy equilibrium, you are not going to be effective in your business and career or, ultimately, in your personal life.

But here's a business reality that pits the ideal against the reality: It is much easier (with fewer serious consequences) later than earlier in a career to say no. So, as you start out and as you are developing your career, you may have to accept doing a lot of things you'd rather not do because, by saying no, you may well be written off for advancement. During those times when you are faced with priorities affecting your personal life, equilibrium, job security, and conflicting career development, you need to pause and act in enlightened self-interest. It is a constant balancing act.

We live in a 24/7/365 business world, and the demands always to "be on" are intense, especially as you move up the ladder. It gets to the point—at least it did for me—that you can never walk down the street or board a plane without looking "presentable" because you might (and will) meet people important to you or your company who expect your best. Send an email and you get a response, which earns you another email with attendant work. (Whom are you helping?) I am not good at saying no, but over the past six or eight years there were so many requests for a piece of me, I simply could not be everywhere and do it all. I had to step back, give up a few things, and set up some rules to protect my life. Sounds dramatic, but it was just coming to reason . . . later rather than sooner. Learn early the strategic use of the word "no": it will serve you well, and more often than not earn you respect.

. . . .

CHOOSE THE RIGHT COMPANY FOR YOU

The most enlightened career decision you can make is working at the right kind of company for you. I don't mean simply the decision of whether to toil at a large corporation or a small one as a step on your way upward or to focus in one business sector versus another, to grow with a start-up or with an established firm. That's just running a pros-and-cons list against the opportunities at hand and an opportunity you'd like in, say, three years.

. . . .

During the first half of your career, the enlightened move is to pick the company(ies) with the most added value for you. In four out of five cases, it is best to avoid no-names whenever possible. Tough but true. But what's in a name, Shakespeare said. There are names and there are names, and the key is to know what those names can mean in connection to *your* future. This book is published by Atria Books of Simon & Schuster. In many contexts, that name doesn't mean anything; if you are in publishing, however, that name is a gold standard. Ever heard of Joël Robuchon or Jean-Georges Vongerichten? If you don't have an interest in food and fine dining, you probably haven't heard of them. In fact, they are two of the world's greatest chefs, each with a venerated upscale international restaurant empire. If you are a young chef and work for one of them in one of their kitchens, you have worked for a name that opens doors.

I appreciate that the necessity of getting a job, any job, intervenes from time to time—life has a way of doing that—but over time you can shape and should shape your employment history effectively.

As someone who has read far too many résumés in her lifetime, I can tell you that I always looked at two things as quick facts to help weed out candidates. Isn't that what reading résumés is all about? Getting from one hundred to ten, then to five as quickly as possible? I looked at the companies where the applicant worked and the school(s) where s/he went. Those two facts live with you forever, and are telling.

Cover letter? I'll level with you, especially in those years when I would bring home shopping bags full of applications on weekends, I often did not read the cover letters when I was making the quick cut to get to the ten most viable candidates. A quick look at their CV and they passed the smell test or did not. And I'll tell you now what I could not tell you then: The résumé generally gave me an idea of the person's age. And we almost always had an acceptable age range in mind when we posted a position. Sometimes it was the age of their supervisor that shaded our decision, sometimes it was simply that the position called for yeoman work best suited for the young and up-and-coming. And, of course, a lot of positions required a modicum of life experiences and gray hair. All of that was unstated but important. Faced with a stack of a hundred cover letters, some running pages long, I may have glanced at some the first go-round, but I read them carefully only when I was considering whom to interview first from the selected group. That's when a well-written, insightful, striking cover letter that shows your personality, a glimpse of the quality of your mind, and specifically what you can bring to the company really matters.

Fact of life: A degree from certain "brand-name," quality universities worldwide (they number about a hundred) is a competitive advantage, at least in the early rounds of interviews. These names open doors to jobs, graduate programs, and networking. If you have that credential, great, but you are only as good as your last degree and your last job. Working for a company in your field that looks good on your résumé, however, is a valuable and attainable goal.

Having worked at a highly respected firm in your industry says a lot about you, including that you've already passed a good number of tests and cleared a number of hurdles. Plus, you probably have received a reasonable amount of training at the expense of your previous employer. Good companies always have good employee development programs.

Okay, so you didn't go to an elite school and you don't have a brand-name company in your neighborhood. Is all lost? Hardly. Everything's relative. And not everyone in America wants to live and work in New York or Chicago or L.A. or be a vice president or CEO. You can further build and leverage your education and develop your work history to your competitive advantage. It is in your enlightened self-interest.

There are plenty of local companies that provide added value appeal. I am sure there are, say, accounting firms that are highly respected in the business community and profession, regionally or globally, that I have never heard of, but on your résumé would be impressive. The same is true for colleges. I bet there are one or two or ten schools that are outside my experience with highly regarded accounting programs that would stand out on your résumé; indeed, some of the people doing the hiring at some of your most desirable firms probably went there. Perhaps you can pick up a graduate degree or a postgrad certificate from one of these programs to add to your credentials. Adding more education can also be part of reinventing yourself, perhaps changing fields or responsibilities within your field. During periods of economic slowdowns or worse, a lot of people choose the route of more education to reinvent themselves. It works. And more education doesn't only mean more advanced training or professional studies, it can mean a broader liberal education, as in philosophy, the arts, cultural studies, or even travel, so you have more to say in business and life than the quickest answer to a quantitative question.

Think local if that's your predilection. Think global if you want to. But, if you want to become the junior senator from the State of New York, you will have to move to New York as someone we all know did, an enlightened self-interest move for someone who wanted ultimately a Washington, D.C., address. You must be willing to relocate!

Working at a strong company with good people helps you learn and grow. My company became a breeding ground for talent and one of the image and performance leaders in the wine business. We trained our people well, and when they were blocked by others for promotion or the headhunters came calling and the money was too good not to consider, many parted over the years. I never took it personally, though perhaps a few left because of the demands I and others made on them. I was happy for them. The opportunities came because of where they worked and the work they had the opportunity to do.

I had not considered until this moment how many of the people who worked for me are presidents of companies today or hold significant positions. It is gratifying. It is also a proof that it is valuable to work for a company that you are proud to list on your résumé. I cannot emphasize that enough. It is in your enlightened self-interest. And let me state again, but more directly, that I am not saying that working for a name company or going to a name school is necessarily going to bring a better or more fulfilling experience. Rather, when it comes to moving forward in your career, you need to be aware that certain names have the power to open doors for you. The important thing is to know what names open what doors, and which doors lead to the best places for you.

. . . .

CHOOSE THE RIGHT POSITION

Only you know what your current dream position is, but there are paths to it and there are dead ends. If you want to be a magazine or book editor, then starting out as an administrative or an editorial assistant after a brand-name college education is the well-worn path. To become the editor in chief, though, you'll need to pick up some facility with numbers as well as words. The higher up you go—from manager of X to director of X to vice president of X—the more bottom-line and revenue encounters of the profit-and-loss kind will factor into your "promotability."

Some simple advice and a periodic reminder: You need to be looking at where the position you are holding or taking can ultimately lead you—it is not a permanent stop, it is a stepping-stone, if you are so inclined. So the "right position" isn't necessarily just what feels good today, but what can prepare you for tomorrow.

More women today are becoming doctors and lawyers than ever before, as I noted in the introduction, when once they would have become nurses and teachers. However, in the corporate world, women are still two to three times more likely to work in service areas and in staff jobs in PR, HR, communications, and the like, where starting out as an assistant is the route to manager and not the breeding ground for CEOs or COOs. If you see yourself as someone higher than a first-rung vice president (of course, a perfectly rewarding position to many), the enlightened move is to gain some operating experience in a position with bottom-line responsibilities and a direct tie to revenue generation. Just a fact of business life.

....

AN ENCORE STAGE

Everything has its season (or stage), and after many years of corporate life, I knew I wanted to cultivate my own garden. I said I have lived a charmed business life, and nearly a decade before it happened, I had my eye on an early retirement date, which happily I missed by staying only six months longer than planned. I had learned a lot and knew a lot, including that there are types of business leaders and executives best suited to certain business situations, and I am a brand builder by temperament and ability. By then, our flagship brand Veuve Clicquot had gone from less than 1 percent U.S. market share to more than 25 percent. We literally had no more Champagne to sell, and most of our two dozen other wine brands were hitting their numbers without much more upside potential. What opened a new door and ushered me into a new phase was not something anyone could have predicted, though it took action on my part, again affirming that you cannot always time or create your opportunities, yet nothing begets nothing. I wrote a book.

....

I had written some magazine pieces over the years, and countless reports, and told lots of instructive stories, and gained a lot of experience and some wisdom. But who wants to publish a first-time book author? With a little management and marketing skill, I was able to make things work out . . . better than anyone could have predicted.

My first book, *French Women Don't Get Fat,* became a number one bestseller in the United States and around the world, and something of a cultural phenomenon, perhaps best exemplified by inspiring not one but two cartoons in *The New Yorker.* It served both me and Champagne Veuve Clicquot very well indeed. Suddenly everyone wanted to talk to me, interview me, or offer me new opportunities. I moved on to a so-called encore career, but I see it as simply a new stage in life. I don't even have or want a title on my business card anymore, but when asked on forms (or wherever) to state my profession, I now write "author" or "writer." It took some time to convince myself of the legitimacy of doing that–I am not Edith Wharton–but I figure three books and a hundred articles qualify me. Lesson: I could never have predicted this career or stage ten years ago. When I was in my twenties and thirties, it never approached the long-term radar screen. Did I act with enlightened self-interest? Sure . . . as soon as I saw the light.

4

OF VELVET GLOVES, WORDS,
AND HANDSHAKES

Can you imagine (or remember) business without Power-Point (or text messaging for that matter)? I would be happy never to see another PowerPoint presentation, though I confess, when they are good they can be a powerful communications tool. But they are mostly bad, and say quite a bit about the presenter. I am always amused by well-meaning people who try to show off by using PowerPoint—cramming their slides with all sorts of information, using much of the available real estate, and thereby forgetting their audience, failing to highlight their points (isn't that the point of PowerPoint?) and violating the all-important rule, Keep it simple (or, in business speak, KISS—Keep it simple, stupid).

Sooner or later, most businesspeople have to make their first major presentation, perhaps pitching a client, speaking at a conference, or internally to an audience that includes their boss, senior colleagues, perhaps the boss's boss. Year in, year out, the latest and greatest version of PowerPoint or another graphics software package gets fired up and we're off to another slide show.

Here's a vintage Jacques and Jill went up the corporate hill story. Back in 2000, Jill worked for us as a manager of communications and marketing and was charged with making a presentation at our national sales conference on integrating our Halloween special events with sales, PR, and merchandizing actions, while protecting and promoting the brand image.

We produced our own PowerPoint slides in-house, sometimes helping each other out with the bells and whistles, and I always thoroughly reviewed the deck before it was presented. I did not want surprises, embarrassments, or time wasted at our annual sales meeting. And I wanted to help prepare and protect people. I would send notes on the deck or meet with the presenter, and the comments often went like this: "Can you bullet that in three words?" "Remember, slides support, not replace you." I would say in my most encouraging voice, "Make the point, then repeat it with a slide." I'd note when there were too many words or points on a slide and suggest presenting them in two or three slides. Yet there were almost always too many slides, so I'd invite people to revisit the key ideas they were trying to get across and perhaps eliminate slides that would add too much extraneous or distracting information. I did not push too hard, but would often ask, "How about a clever graphic here?" "Any audio clips to liven it up?" "Would it be better to fly the points in or give each one its own slide?" And I always checked that they had good illustrations so people were not always staring at text. My final piece of advice was always the same: Rehearse what you think is your final version, preferably out loud to someone, a couple of days before you deliver it.

Call it mentoring or enlightened self-interest (mine) or both and more, because if Jill delivered a great presentation, we both looked good. And she did. (And if she hadn't, at least she would not have to worry about the boss being upset with her; we were in it together, and I had already assumed some of the responsibility for her presentation.) Her presentation was so good, in fact, that I invited her to give the talk in France at our next global communications and marketing meeting.

Jacques gave a presentation at that global meeting as well. He held a position comparable to Jill's in France, and was similarly in his late twenties or early thirties and was making an important presentation to an audience of about fifty, most well above him in rank. (At meetings like this, I was always amused that the boss or bosses typically assigned presentations to everyone below them, rarely to themselves. Easy. I always gave myself a presentation . . . until one day I didn't. After a while, I questioned what I was proving and why I forced the extra work on myself.)

Well, Jacques's presentation was awful. It looked okay. In France, managers are not particularly hands-on, so they would, of course, send out the text to a media company for the preparation of the visuals. So, while the slides were reasonably slick, the media company wasn't asked to edit Jacques's talk but just to make the slides he requested . . . thus, garbage in, garbage out. Jacques's points were made in sentences, which he read, along with everyone else. The slides added little and were monotonous. And though they looked good, they did not fool anyone into thinking they had much content. End result? Everyone labeled Jill as "high potential," and Jacques as inexperienced and weak. As I see it in the rearview mirror, he had potential (though with a bit of French know-it-all arrogance, or was that a sign of insecurity and self-defense?), but he was untutored and unprepared and simply left exposed by his bosses to hang in the breeze. Within a few years, Jill was a vice president and Jacques was working for another company.

Face it, in business, communication skills are the key to a successful career, more than intelligence, knowledge, or experience. The latter might get you the job, but the former gets you promoted. Really. Leadership skills are important, too, but a good deal of what goes into being a leader are good skills at communicating. (And you thought it was what, education?) It used to be that a bachelor's degree was the entry card to the career ladder game, and it still can be, though the expectation of an advanced degree has become the standard in corporate America and beyond. I suppose if you have an MBA or a master's in an appropriate specialty, you might be able to do financial math or strategic analysis a tad better and give a more conventional, formulaic presentation of your ideas than someone without as much academic experience, but I must say, I have hired MBAs (I don't have one) who were "innocent" coming out of top business schools. There's truth to the corporate mantra, "Do well in school, then we'll teach you what you need to know the first year on the job." I certainly learned by doing on the job.

The quality that sets people apart in business is their ability to communicate orally, in small and large settings, their ability to write effectively—to get their points across clearly and efficiently in a variety of forms to a variety of audiences—and to communicate visually, whether through graphic (as in charts and graphs), pictorial (as in arresting photographs or drawings), or verbal (such as bullet points or pithy stories, or even word pictures and graphs) messages. Dynamic businesspeople also have the ability to work collaboratively in crafting various forms of verbal and nonverbal communication. *Le savoir faire avec le faire savoir* (communication) *permet l'efficacité.*

....

THE POWER OF HELLO

Communication is about much more than presentation. It is something we do constantly throughout the day, every time we come in contact with another person. First things first. How's your handshake? We're all told to have a firm handshake. As a petite woman in a man's business world, I practiced "the iron fist in a velvet glove" approach. I shook hands with vigor, meaning I more or less squeezed (not bone-crunchingly hard . . . I did not have that ability). That startled a few and got me taken seriously. And I always looked them straight in the eye (an almost lost art

....

in our multitasking world). It was a message I needed to send, especially early in my career.

As you probably know, the origin of the handshake was a sign of friendship; the parties were showing that they were not holding weapons. Well, a good salutation is a powerful mood, tone, and conversation setter. It is also a social equalizer. The power of looking men (and women) in the eye and smiling is enormous, and the consequences of not doing so are equally telling and consequential.

I once had a boss who each morning marched through the office with his cardboard cup of coffee and briefcase and looked neither right nor left, did not say hello or smile. Perhaps an hour or so later, he would emerge from his room and behave civilly. He was a good professional, surely a night and not a morning person, but there was no reason or excuse for setting such an example, because when it comes from a person in authority, it tends to pervade the culture of the organization. His mornings did not promote employee retention, loyalty to him, or productivity.

Arguably the most important word in the French language is *bonjour*—hello—or literally, "good" (*bon*) "day" (*jour*). What's so tough about saying a pleasant hello with a smile to the people with whom you work? It is so much a part of French culture and etiquette that it is unthinkable to walk into a shop of any kind and not exchange *bonjour* as the first order of business. Not to do so is considered rude, and in this service economy we live in, you have a much better chance of being treated nicely and well if you start off your day, meeting, or exchange with a sincere hello.

Let me say again: Look people in the eyes. And learn their

names. That takes a little effort, but when you address people by name, it makes a difference. Even "Good morning, Jim," trumps "Good morning." "Jim's idea is a good one" earns points over "That idea is good." Think about yourself on the receiving end. Suddenly it is friendly and personal, not perfunctory or cold. Don't you like those people? I remember a "famous" restaurant critic to whom I was introduced several times over the course of a year or two. Each time she asked me my name. I am sure she knew it, because one time I sat across from her at dinner, but it was a little power thing for her.

THE POWER OF THANK YOU IN ANY LANGUAGE

Thank you is obviously another powerful communications phrase and tool. People like to be thanked, though we overdo the superlatives. A good job is a job well done. Not every performance is or has to be great. Today if you want to stand out in business, write thank-you notes. People remember. I don't mean a quick email. That's better than not sending one at all, and certainly has its place and is appropriate in many contexts, but imagine getting a handwritten note of thanks or congratulations from someone. A lost art and practice? It makes a statement. Is life so full that there's no time to thank or praise people? Are we so stressed and hurried that we do not make the effort to acknowledge people who impact on our personal or professional lives?

Before you think I am some nineteenth-century relic, let me

assure you I get it that to communicate effectively involves considering your audience/receiver and taking appropriate measures to connect the sender and receiver so the intended message is received. For some, email is already too last century or too baby boomerish a medium. Today's Millennials, the Gen Yers, would text a thank-you after a meeting: *Thx. C U soon.* Short, to the point, and not long-winded, though almost anyone born before, say, 1946 would perhaps take exception with its abruptness and impersonality and informality. Recognizing differences in communications styles and bridging the communications gap is an emerging challenge in the workplace.

What I want to share is that writing personalized thank-yous is one of those old-world practices that has served me well and distinguished my practice of business, and perhaps would for you, too. Increasingly, it stands out and gets noticed, of course partly because it is done less and less. I write dozens and dozens of notes a year, and have done so my entire adult life. It adds up. Some of the best business contacts I made came from so-called cold-call congratulatory notes I sent after reading or hearing about someone's success. It helped, of course, when I included a bottle of Champagne with the note. I did not expect anything specific in return, but over time, sometimes years, a lot of those contacts produced a return.

One early January morning, maybe ten years ago, I was walking past the office of a young sales manager as he was busy writing greeting cards. He perked up when he saw me and proudly showed me one from his little stack (implicitly saying, I've learned your lesson and how to distinguish our company's approach). The card read: "Thank you for your support. I really appreciate it." And he signed his name in illegible male executive scrawl. Here was an intelligent young man who was great at sales and had wonderful presence and rapport with his customers, sending the same formulaic message to each of his major clients. Should I let this happen? After a little ever so important warm-up chitchat, I said to him, "Roger, how would you feel getting a card like this?" He paused and looked at the card and said, "Oh, I'll add Dear So-and-So later." "Okay, one point. But what about your message?" This smart chap smiled and was getting it. (Of course, delivering constructive criticism is tricky and can be received simply as criticism, especially if it comes from your boss or higher, but if you know your audience you can tailor your approach.) "How can you personalize it? Each of your customers is unique, and since you see them regularly, you must know something about them that could shape up your message," I continued. "Point taken," he said, and I asked if he knew that the owners of a major account in Connecticut were off to a resort for a few days of rest. He did. "In that case, how about sending flowers or a bottle of Champagne to their rooms with a personal and relevant note? They are, after all, one of our leading restaurant customers." His smile widened and he took up a new stack and started "personalizing" his notes.

A few months later, I went to that restaurant, and the chef came out of the kitchen to tell me and my guests how proud I should be for having such wonderful staff, and that no one at any other wine or food company had made the effort to send him and his wife such a touching note, and a timely gift as well. His wife, the front-of-the-house manager, had already greeted us with effusive thanks. How many times do you think they would remember or tell the story? What do you think the impact was on their relationship with our company? Sales doubled and image rose. I went back to the office the next day and told Roger that whatever he did for this couple, he now had friends for life. He smiled again. As Oprah rightly says, "Everybody wants to feel appreciated."

I know this note-writing technique continues to work well, because it just did for me again, for the 923,848,475th time (give or take a few digits). A journalist in Baltimore whom I've never met wrote a nice little piece about my approach to food and life that was forwarded to me by a friend. So, I pulled out a copy of the new edition of *French Women for All Seasons Engagement Calendar,* dedicated it to her, wrote a few lines of thanks, and had it sent. Within the month I was surprised to see another piece by the journalist devoting half her column to my personal note and the gift I'd sent, for which she thanked me publicly, with a further appreciation for my work, including mention of both my *French Women* books. It confirmed the meaning of public relations.

Professionally and personally, I have sent gifts to many people each year, and I am stunned by how few formal thank-yous I get in return. No phone call, email, written note . . . nothing. Sometimes, the next time I see a person, they remember to say thanks . . . but only a few. Our mailman always sends us a handwritten thank-you card for our relatively modest holiday gift. Those who do write a note stand out and are remembered.

N'est-ce pas? Everyone who has worked for me was always encouraged to say thank you, thank you, and thank you.

....

LANGUAGES

I've said that communication skills are the key to a successful career. We all must know and exploit our best communication assets. Maybe your best asset is the ability to write brilliant memos or humorous and effective emails, or to present complex financial matters clearly and simply, or to give presentations, or perhaps to be an entertaining lunch date. Know thyself. Whatever it is, you need to recognize it and exploit it. Be the person you are. Work with what you have. In my case, and in retrospect, my greatest talent is the ability to speak my native language. Really. (I recognize that is not a business skill that can be learned, but a lot of communication skills can be developed.) My professional breaks came because I was a presentable French woman in New York who spoke English and French equally proficiently, both with an authentic French accent. If I were in Paris, I would not have stood out. Everything has context. It helped that I was reasonably well educated, had good business and social experiences on both sides of the Atlantic, and had (and have) a passion for food, wine, and travel. But, honestly, it was my ability to communicate orally and in writing in English and French (and some other languages) that distinguished me time after time.

When a Chinese-American friend sent his gorgeous daughter, Valery, to me for some career advice, and I took inventory of

....

her interests and skills, I was startled that this American-raised and -educated daughter of Chinese-born parents did not even mention in her résumé that she speaks Chinese, but proudly cited her French skills and experience, garnered through college and exchange programs. In today's global economy, do you think the ability to communicate in Chinese and English is an asset? How about Chinese, English, and French? Now, there's an impressive calling card in many business sectors. Add good looks, a professional demeanor, and a good education, *et voilà*, as we say in French. Today she is a successful corporate attorney.

Well, we cannot all be born French or Chinese, but we can learn French or Chinese or Spanish or Arabic or whatever. Learn the language and learn the culture, and through travel and exchange learn the business etiquette. Surprisingly, in this digital age, it turns out languages and culture are increasingly important in the global economy, and one thing I do know firsthand is that the emerging professionals in China, the Middle East, Eastern Europe, and beyond, all speak at least two languages well—their native language and English. And if someday you find yourself in one of those countries, as I found myself in America, your native fluency in English will be one of your distinguishing characteristics, provided other language and communication skills are solid.

....

THE GENTLE ART OF CONVERSATION

The gift of good conversation is an extremely valuable though greatly underrated and underdeveloped business skill. The abil-

....

ity to make conversation is as much a skill as being a good negotiator or knowing how to read a P&L. Even more so, in my opinion. Here's where women often excel but do not exploit their talent. You need to be able to tell a good story, be sensitive to the use of "I" and "me" in them, and add some humor. Worry about your audience, not yourself. Good stories command the listener's or reader's attention, are enjoyable, and are remembered. I always made a practice of telling a story as a "teaching moment" with staff. Start lecturing someone and their eyes fog over or their mind jumps to other foci—"What did I do wrong? . . . This woman is a dragon. . . . How much longer is this boring stuff going to last?"—or a thousand other divergent thoughts, not all sweet, as you can imagine. I just wanted to make my point in a way that would make them recognize it for themselves and remember it. Learn to tell stories to illustrate points. I hope a few of the stories in this book do just that.

Let's take another instance of the distinguishing merits of being a good conversationalist—the legendary success in the men's world of doing business on the golf course. What is that about? It is certainly a largely male bastion where women rarely are invited or succeed. At its simplest, it is about developing one-on-one or small-group relationships, since people do business with people and then possibly buy from people they know and like. It is about escaping the office and another meeting in a conference room in exchange for some fresh air and movement. But mostly it is about telling stories, having a few laughs, and enjoying conversation, only a token amount, that relates explicitly or implicitly to today's business. It's no surprise that top salesmen and business development types spend a lot of their "working hours" on the golf course, entertaining or participating in corporate events. And the golf score doesn't matter . . . but the nineteenth hole does.

Some women try to behave like men and succeed on the golf course, but if that's not you, what do you do? What if you are not the type to sit around hotel bars and strike up conversations? (Who is?) Cultivate your own opportunities for conversation. For me, that meant entertaining a great deal over lunch or dinner, and also creating other entertainment opportunities. Not everyone can host parties in their home, but I often created social environments for my staff and customers—a night out at Cirque du Soleil or at the theater (instead of a sporting event). Large corporations create major corporate events, as we often did, but in cultivating good conversation and good business relationships for yourself, create your own settings, and don't limit yourself to inviting only people in your established environment or immediate future. Nothing wrong with getting to know competitors if it is not on the corporate nickel, or meeting friends of friends whose degree of separation from helping your business and career often turns out to be less than six degrees. This may sound like Networking 101, but my point is that you need to place yourself in an environment where your good conversational skills can help distinguish you. In my experience, a dozen good, well-rehearsed personal stories and a few jokes go a long way, just like a good haircut and a glass of Champagne.

If you have already passed Networking 101 (and I don't mean in engineering school), you can skip this paragraph and the next two. But because networking in business is so important and for many an underdeveloped *communication* skill that works (see Maria's story in chapter 1 as proof . . . and my story as well), I want to share just three thoughts on it here, especially as it follows logically on building good conversational skills, and I get asked about it a lot by women in the early stages of their careers. But first, *à ma façon*, a little prefatory anecdote.

A few years ago I was asked by an editor of the online edition of the *New York Times* to engage in a Q&A. Lots of people posted questions for me to answer. One amusing chap wondered if I had any advice on how he could win a French woman's heart. Well, I did. "It seems to me you have to start by finding a French woman," I wrote, and "France isn't a bad place to start. They have a lot of single French women, and the food isn't bad, either." Networking is not a passive sport. You need to get to the people you want to meet, and it takes planning and work and overcoming inertia.

No doubt you've already been told to target business breakfasts, industry conferences, cocktail parties, trade events; do lunch; bring lots of business cards because you are building your contact list. Whom do you want to meet? Women business leaders? Go to a women's business conference or at least go to a talk by a business leader who is a woman. Networking is not a one-time event, so go to something regularly, at least once a month or once a quarter. When you are there, talk. Ask questions. Use your conversational skills. Make eye contact, smile, and introduce yourself in a not-too-aggressive fashion to anyone who is not sending stay-away signals. Join a group, say, "Hello, I'm (fill in your name)." Seriously, most people appreciate the rules of the game of networking. If you can introduce someone to someone else, do it. If you picked the wrong person or group, fade away after a bit and start over. Be graceful and sensitive so that you don't appear to be a bore or shark.

How do you meet Mrs. Big? She's used to people coming up to her, so go ahead. And say something intelligent that requires a response that could begin a conversation. "I've been thinking what you said about A, B, or C, and I wonder if (fill in the blank)." You've got one chance. And don't overstay your welcome. If you've made a good impression, you may get an invitation to send her an email or call her office. But here's a secret: Famous people often will prolong a conversation with someone they are enjoying speaking with to avoid another and another and another person coming up and speaking to them. You might get lucky. See, networking is easy, *très facile,* and here are my three thoughts again: Go, Talk, Behave. *Bonne chance.*

PAINT YOURSELF ORANGE

Be Your Own Brand: Part I

Today, Champagne Veuve Clicquot, with its striking orange label, is one of the best known and regarded "wines" in America and the world over. In 1984, when I took charge of Veuve Clicquot's marketing in the United States, however, the Champagne had been imported for more than two hundred years, with the same importer for more than one hundred years, and its market share was less than 1 percent. It wasn't a brand that mattered much, despite its rich history, including the remarkable story of Madame Clicquot, whose motto—"One quality, the finest"—continues to define the company's culture and operations. At that time in the American market, Clicquot had a schizophrenic distribution network that needed fixing, but that was no surprise, because it did not have its brand identity and messaging down.

If you are not a brand, you are a commodity, and Champagne Veuve Clicquot fell into the broad commodity market of sparkling wines, along with tens of millions of bottles from Italy, America, and Spain as well as France on retail shelves and on wine lists. And in America, where almost anything that bubbles can be and is called Champagne (something that's illegal in most other countries), you did not even have as a given the fact that Veuve Clicquot came from the Champagne region of France, ninety miles northeast of Paris. (Veuve Clicquot has the sort of famous name that some people think they know, and I was startled on many occasions when people cited it as a wine from Bordeaux.)

At many weddings there is a "Champagne toast," though probably more than 99 percent of the time, people are not toasting with real Champagne (there simply isn't enough for that). Plus, there were another 130 Champagnes from the region exported to America, from tiny productions from growers who bottled their own harvests to large cooperatives to the great houses, including Moët, the world volume leader by far.

Given all this, how was I to establish Veuve Clicquot as a front-of-the-mind brand and image leader? In addition, there was a special challenge. Even though not many people knew its name and that it was Champagne and not, say, a still wine or something completely different, seemingly no one born outside France could pronounce its name, Veuve Clicquot (vuv klee-'ko). And if people felt uncomfortable saying its name, they certainly would not order it. That was a problem.

With such a small market share and thus modest revenue, we did not have much money for advertising and communications, certainly not enough for the necessary repeat advertising insertions in top magazines that all the leading global brands buy, especially in the luxury category that has affinities with Champagne. Big-time events with paid guest stars that generate PR were unaffordable. TV and video were out for lots of reasons. So what to do?

One day I hit on the idea of radio. This was in 1985, and a higher percentage of people listened to radio in their cars or at home at the start and end of the business day than today. I thought, what better way than on radio to tell the story of Veuve Clicquot and repeat the name (klee-'ko . . . I know, I begin to sound like an ad for a brand I no longer work for). I spoke with a radio account executive in New York, and he agreed with the radio tactic and confirmed that it could be done with a modest budget.

First we needed thirty- and sixty-second radio spots as part of a radio campaign. And before we could do that (and here "we" was simply me, as we could not afford a New York ad agency, endless focus groups, et cetera), we needed to get our positioning and messaging down. Luckily, Veuve Clicquot is a great world brand and at the time it was strong, as it is today, in England, Germany, and Italy, so the messages were out there, just not codified in a way to differentiate the brand—what I came to call the Clicquot difference. I fixed on three or four points, depending on how you count, because when it comes to core messaging and core values, you cannot go on and on. You need a few, and everything needs to show them and support them. Your brand is a promise, so you need to be objective and clever.

The first message and differentiating point was VCP's (Veuve Clicquot Ponsardin's—the brand's full name, Ponsardin being Madame Clicquot's maiden name) place in history and culture, especially the story of Madame Clicquot, a widow who took over her husband's position, created many firsts in Champagne, and grew her Champagne house to world fame and prosperity. She distinguishes the VCP brand from other Champagnes; they cannot tell her story.

The second characteristic was quality, which included such proof points as especially great vineyard holdings, a history of great winemakers, and, of course, the longtime Clicquot motto, *"une qualité . . . la toute première . . .* one quality, the finest." I also raised the price to the highest among nonvintage Champagnes, which signaled quality to people ("It must be very good at that price"). For most products there is usually the highest-priced and frequently presumed quality leader, the lowest-priced brand, and often a brand perceived as the value leader. I wanted VCP to be known as the quality and image leader, and we had the quality in the bottle to back up that positioning.

VCP's label is one of its best communication tools and brand identifiers. Its flagship nonvintage brut is called *Carte Jaune,* or in English, "Yellow Label," where the color is egg yolk yellow (or what used to be the color of egg yolks when all chickens were free-range). We began using that color for everything, literally painting the town yellow. Over time we tried to "own" the color orange (the look-alike equivalent of egg yolk yellow), before it became a "hot" color. Perhaps we had a little to do with the fashion world's embracing it. Soon we were running Yelloween parties all over for Halloween. In a classic bit of integrated marketing before any of us knew the term, we owned all the wine shop windows the week of October 31, just when the year-end Champagne season kicks off, and were feting our best trade and consumer customers at our events just at that moment. That distinguished us from other brands. Go with your strengths and opportunities, especially when you can stand out from the competition and they cannot respond. It is true in fashion, in food, presumably in lawn mowers. Macy's "owns" the Thanksgiving Day Parade. Decades and decades ago they could have paid to brand any major parade, but they were savvy and innovative enough to support a parade that gets their department store's name before the entire nation via television and to a lesser degree radio and print, at the precise moment of the biggest shopping weekend and the start of the biggest shopping month of the year. It was a great move in its time.

My compound problem was that people still had to be able to pronounce the name. So, armed with my messages of the Clicquot difference, notably VPC's place in history and culture ("Pushkin wrote about it"; "it is the Champagne of *Casablanca*"; and the story of "The Widow" Clicquot, the world's first modern businesswoman, the orange label, and "one quality, the finest"), I was ready for a radio spot.

The kind account executive suggested I go to an old legend in radio and communications, Tony Schwartz, who did some advertising consulting and production. "What's your purpose, who is your audience, how much have you got to spend?" he asked in his New York way.

The purpose was easy: Get people to know the brand and pronounce its name. Create a "pull." Get people to ask for and buy the Champagne. The audience wasn't hard to define, though it was years and years before we had proper research evidence. I said, "People from twenty-five to fifty-five who can afford a bottle of Champagne and go out to restaurants and events, probably in major metropolitan areas." At the time a bottle of Yellow Label cost a bit less than $20 (today, $40+), so it was an affordable luxury, but our customers needed some disposable income.

It did not take long for us to settle on classical radio stations as our first outlet. "Their ad rates are lower than rock and contemporary stations'," Tony said, "and their audience is wealthier." And I thought classical music sent the right quality and culture image that is part of VCP's brand identity. Okay. We still needed the spots.

Tony and two copywriters wrote a few versions of our story, and when I went to hear them, he said, "We think they should be read by a woman with a French accent. Would you read a few sound tests so we can see how it works?" I did not have much choice, and so I read, take after take, as they cut words and tweaked phrases to fit into thirty- and sixty-second spots. Like most people, I did not much recognize or care for the sound of my own voice, but the pros there liked the spots. We were ready to hire the talent with a French accent to record them.

A week later, Tony said, "You know, we are looking for someone to sound like you; why don't you record them?" "Absolutely not," I said to myself and him. I thought, Are these people crazy? What would the chairman and president back in France think about me as the voice of Veuve Clicquot on the radio? I am no egomaniac. Quite the opposite. I did not want to expose myself to accusations of self-promotion and more. "Your voice is perfect . . . we can't find any as good as you . . ." "In this city with some of the greatest actors in the world?" I responded. "But they are acting, you are not," and so on and so on.

A month later I recorded three radio commercials. The clincher was, I did not have to pay for someone to record the spots. (I always treated the company's money as if it were my own, and if I could save a little, I did, to use it another day.) The ads first ran on WQXR, the classical radio station of the *New York Times*, to very favorable results. The campaign had "great legs," and over the next fifteen years, I recorded another thirty spots along the very same lines, and as VCP's sales and marketing budgets grew, we added more classical music stations, then jazz, then news stations.

Other brands took notice, of course. No other Champagne and to my knowledge no other premium wine had ever advertised on radio, which again distinguished our brand, but some soon did. And since stations who wanted our repeat business were sensitive to accepting ads from competitors, I generally was consulted on all wine placements, and I made sure no other Champagne advertised on the stations where we did. That's when I learned the phrase "a good offense is the best defense."

One of the more aggressive uses we made of the radio campaign turned out to be a brilliant piece of luck. Radio spots cost the most in the fall weeks leading up to Christmas. Then, for a week or so, radio advertising falls off precipitously, as does the cost. Well, those days are precisely when the greatest number of bottles of Champagne are sold each year, leading up to and including New Year's Eve. So, with a few hints from a friendly account executive with a taste for Champagne, I had the idea to make a preemptive low-ball offer to a major radio network to buy a great many spots across their entire network during the week starting December 26 . . . and won. For a truly modest fee, we were everywhere across the United States, the Caribbean, and beyond. People from a wide range of demographics had the name *Veuve Clicquot* on their minds just when they were about to consume the only bottle of Champagne they predictably drank each year. It worked so well, we bought time on a second major radio network the next year.

Life is lived in episodes or seasons, as I've said, and the season of radio has changed since then, so eventually this brand-building exercise was phased out, though not before we had obtained 25 percent of the Champagne market in America.

An amusing sidelight for me to all of this was that my voice became well known. I got offers from other luxury brands to do more voice-overs (which I declined), and numerous times when I met a person for the first time at a party or over the phone, they'd pause and say, "*That* voice . . . you know, you sound just like the person in the Veuve Clicquot commercials. . . . You know, that's how I discovered Veuve Clicquot." And I'd smile to myself and think, *Mission accomplie.*

One important takeaway from this brand-building story is to remember that messaging has to be consistent—for fifteen years we "showed" the same three points in many ways, and there needs to be much repetition. You can't change your commercial each year or season if you want to be noticed and remembered. It takes time to become a brand. A lot of money helps to speed things up, but it is not essential.

Lots of brands "refresh" their packaging every few years, which can be as simple as offering new gift boxes and gift bags to inject a bit of energy and freshness. Tweaking a label is a bit more serious if you are working with a well-established "name," because you are playing with the brand's iconic identity. And, of course, a new ad campaign, whether simply in print or including television and all the related collateral materials, is a classic approach to reaching out to new audiences or bringing a brand back to front-of-the-mind awareness. We always made sure we had chic young men and women, especially women, in our VCP ads (appealing to elegance, contemporary good looks, luxury, and, of course, sex), and the look that said all of that had to be refreshed every few years to be "with it." In a sense, that helped us to reinvent ourselves as a Champagne for today (not yesterday), especially as we targeted new consumers just coming of age and getting to know us for the first time. We did not reinvent ourselves in the sense of changing what we are or what was in our bottle. Some companies do that with "new and improved" products or through brand extensions such as a clothing company that comes to be identified as a brand that also sells watches and handbags.

Just as established products and brands need updating to stay alive and vibrant, you periodically need to refresh or reinvent yourself. You can change your packaging with a haircut and new glasses, say, or you can reinvent yourself beyond packaging by changing careers, partners, and perhaps even some deep philosophical approaches to life, including religion. Not surprisingly, perhaps, I vote for changing how you eat.

....

Be Your Own Brand: Part II

What do people think of when they think of *you* as a brand? If you don't stand out with a clear identity, you are lost in a sea of indistinguishable peers. If you have business ambitions, you don't want to be a commodity, something perceived as commonly available, unspecialized and easily exchangeable with another product of the same type. If you are the only woman in the room, you'll usually be noticed, unless you are a woman who is a commodity, an interchangeable performer.

You need to be known for your unique qualities, and that means being recognized. Your brand needs to be known for its unique offerings and differentiating factors. What traits make you stand out?

We all live with "sensory-overloaded" hearts and minds. Getting a properly refined message through the clutter requires scrupulous use of every resource over the long term. The uniform look, sound, and feel of a product and brand, expressed through all its activities, will do more over time to "seat" a message than the best ad campaign. To say it another way, consistent messaging will support and therefore leverage the campaign. What's your message?

....

YOUR MESSAGE?

In our increasingly digital times, you don't need to launch a radio campaign for yourself to get your message out, but you probably need to consider a good web presence, perhaps a readily accessible digital profile on a professional social network that keeps your business life current, and, of course, many women have their own websites or blogs and use them to promote themselves professionally. However, there are dangers in not doing this right—from unflattering pictures of you to statements you or people have made that you'd like back and are inconsistent with the message you'd like to send. Just remember: Quality in all things, and less is more.

I learned two important lessons early on. I mentioned how I positioned Veuve Clicquot as the most expensive nonvintage Champagne. It has held that position ever since and is now consistently viewed that way around the world. And sales increased. Perception is reality (of course, there was quality and a full-bodied house style in the bottle to support the positioning). The second lesson was that you are judged by whom you hang around with. That is, when Veuve Clicquot is sometimes called the Armani of Champagne, that works for me. If you work for a luxury goods company where perception is reality and image is all-important, you just can't stay in second-class hotels. (I know, that's tough work.) If you are Cartier, your stores must have extremely prestigious addresses. It is all about messaging, in all things. I am not suggesting that you present yourself as something you are not, because a brand is a promise, and you'll have to deliver on your distinguishing characteristics. But be conscious of how you present yourself now and for your next appearance, be it personal or professional.

An important point about messaging—if I say it three times it is true—keep it simple and keep it consistent. I cannot repeat this enough. Most people know there are ten commandments but many cannot name them all. If Moses kept his message to three points—as communication gurus are ready to remind us—he'd certainly have a much greater recall rate.

Again, it is essential and true for all brands (not just for luxury brands) to have a "compelling identity." Deciding who you are as an enterprise and what is unique about your offerings is the first and indispensable branding step. Once defined, that unique selling proposition becomes the rock upon which all else is built.

Building a brand also requires discipline. Again, we have to be consistent. We have to make sure we're saying the same things in the same ways or the brand becomes diluted. And, maybe hardest, we have to do things that support the brand (and stop doing things that don't).

A concept close to my heart is being comfortable in your own skin—*bien dans sa peau*. It is not only part and parcel of achieving balance in business and life, it also relates directly to being your own brand. Being *bien dans sa peau* means being your unique self. It means being true to your unique outward self in addition to your inward, emotional self. It means developing your own style, a look and manner that feels comfortable and right to you and that you present to the world. What's your brand's DNA and how is it expressed? Clothes, jewelry, makeup, hair . . . voice, laugh, touch? I have a good friend who wears a very distinctive color of lipstick. I rarely wear lipstick, but she stands out with her deep, dark shade. I know someone who always wears a large brooch, someone who wears a distinctive religious cross. I could go on. I'll say this about me: scarves, necklaces, sunglasses.

If you are fifty and dress like a twenty-year-old, you are certainly making a brand statement, just as you do if you have carrot-colored hair (which you will see in Paris) or heavy black boots in summer (which you will see in New York . . . as well as flip-flops in dressy or formal settings, which surely can be a brand faux pas, but it does command attention).

Remember the main character in the feel-good movie *Working Girl* (1988)? Secretary and executive-in-the-making Tess McGill (Melanie Griffith) opines, "If you want to get ahead in business . . . you've got to have serious hair." Well, she's right. In *French Women Don't Get Fat*, I wrote, "French women know one can go far with a great haircut, a bottle of Champagne, and a divine perfume." I believe it.

Bad hair is a branding catastrophe for women. If I could give women one "beauty and branding tip," it would be to get a great haircut and invest in regular blow-dries. I am a bit embarrassed by the time and money I have had to spend on my hair over my professional life, but, though it bothers me, it was simply essential. I had to be and wanted to be presentable at all times.

The harsh reality is that women in the workplace are judged on their looks a lot more than men. Say it's not fair, but it is a

silent reality. Face it. Women do not have to be gorgeous to succeed; indeed, there's the argument that being too good-looking
can work against a woman in many professions. A woman, however, needs to be well groomed and presentable, let's call it *soi-
gnée*. Period. Whom do you want to represent your company?
Someone with dirty, stringy hair and/or—dare I say it?—with
an out-of-balance physique? Brains and personality may still get
them hired, but not on the front lines or fast track, I suspect. Ah,
the hair I've seen. Take care of your appearance. And the easiest
way is to get some objective advice about your hair and take
action. You've got to have "serious" hair.

Your appearance makes a nonverbal, emotional appeal, branding statement and often forms the first impression of you. You've
heard the phrase "you don't get a second chance to make a good
first impression." First impressions count in business and in life.

First impressions in business may be by phone or email, but
most important ones—as in a job interview—are still face-to-
face (even if via teleconference) and are visual and nonverbal for
openers. Here, too, my mother had words of wisdom: Remember, it is your hair, your eyes and smile, then your shoes. (Have
you ever felt someone subtly looking you over from head to
foot? I have; it's common.) Somehow, these are the areas where
we seem to focus first and use to make our first and often lasting
assessment of a person's appearance and overall look.

In business, what we wear applies unfairly more to women
than men, as we all know, and different corporate fields and cultures call for different dress standards, including within the
ranks. So, if you are seeking a new position at a new company or

a transfer or promotion within your current one, do research ahead of time on the corporate environment and dress the part.

. . . .

STYLE

Being your own brand means you have a style. While that style may fit generally into an established category, your individual style also sets you apart from others in this group or class. The trick is to stand out favorably within the bounds of appropriateness, in most contexts and especially on business occasions.

A lot of people assume French women have an innate sense of style. Being French, I hear that a lot. Well, yes and no. Sure, French women are imbued with lessons along the way toward adulthood. The lessons and models are everywhere in French culture and society—from advertisements to school uniforms to identifiable behaviors and practices common to French families. I can usually spot a French person in a crowd on any street in any city outside France. They move and look a certain way. But a style is cultivated over time and involves lessons and choices as one matures. It is generally never too late to develop or refine one's unique style. And not everyone gets it right. Imagine that. Some just don't see the consequences of their ways.

Not long ago I was at a corporate meeting, and a French woman in her late forties with little sense of style was making a presentation on the state of her company. She was wearing a dull business suit and I imagine she thought she'd cheer it up with long dangling earrings à la Swarovski, the bling-bling kind.

. . . .

They seemed tacky and inappropriate to me. The only other woman in the room, an Italian with a superb sense of style, shot me a look that said it all. And the men? Their faces were saying sarcastically, What was she thinking? As Coco Chanel put it, "If a woman is not well dressed, one notices her for her outfit, but if she's impeccably dressed, it's she that one notices." In business you don't need or want to draw attention to yourself as a spectacle. When in doubt, be classic and neutral in your attire when making a presentation. Let the content and presentation and "you" distinguish you.

How do you define style? How can a person develop and possess her own style? For me, style is zee whole package: how you dress, talk, move, and behave. It all goes together into that first-impression equation. It shouldn't be confused with chic; an extremely chic or well-dressed woman may have zero sense of style. Style is definitely more about who the person is inside. Confidence and individuality are two strong assets for developing your personal style. Can it be taught? To a certain extent, yes, but at the end of the day it has to do a lot with being *bien dans sa peau*, knowing thyself and having balance in one's life.

. . . .

CLOTHES MAKETH THE WOMAN

As Edith Wharton wrote in *The House of Mirth*, "The clothes are the background, the frame if you like: they don't make success,

. . . .

but they are part of it." Let me provide a short checklist of some of the "no-no's" for presenting oneself if one wants responsible positions on the ladder. (I have seen every one of these mistakes made by "losing" applicants.)

NO:

- ✓ sheer clothing (mostly tops) and deep cleavage (What were they thinking?)

- ✓ strapless tops (anything strapless or "beach" clothing is inappropriate for a city interview and anywhere in most countries and cultures)

- ✓ strong perfume

- ✓ too much makeup

- ✓ flip-flops (even if it's Friday and dreadfully hot and humid) or open-toed, high-heeled strappy shoes

- ✓ chipped nails or fake ones

- ✓ beat-up jeans (and, in my book, any jeans for an interview)

- ✓ dressing like a man, unless you are trying to signal you are one

- ✓ superminiskirts

- ✓ unpressed shirt or unironed anything

✓ unkempt hair

✓ too much jewelry (I'm thinking big hoop earrings on a petite woman)

I think you get the picture. I don't need to add things like runs in stockings or soiled clothing. For that your inner mentor should suffice. What is the brand you are living and projecting? In a few instances, I have heard my male colleagues make interesting biting comments after meeting someone, but we shall not go there. The point is that wearing the right clothes will not alone get you an automatic hire or promotion, but it will earn you respect and appreciation for professionalism. The alternative is bad for your business.

As for the eyes and smile, this is something one can have total control over. Don't overdo your eyes with makeup. (I have seen beautiful young, fair-skinned, and light-haired women in their early twenties with much natural beauty tarnished by heavy dark eye shadow . . . were they trying to look older?) Do look people in the eye with genuine attention; likewise, make your smile sincere. Even if you are nervous, a smile will help you relax and keep your facial features smooth.

What's wearable is not so difficult to judge because the three interrelated golden rules are: Quality over quantity; Simplicity in all things; Less is more (not in the sense of showing off your skin, but in terms of composition).

Many of the women who joined our companies were for a while far from projecting the ideal "luxury" world image (and that does not mean expensive designer clothes). But by observing what colleagues wear and, most important, what the boss or boss's boss wears, one can and will get the picture fast.

A leader leads by example, and as much as I love leggings and a sleeveless T-shirt at home, it was never part of my public appearance, not even during those infamous years of casual Fridays or at casual sales meetings away from the office. One reason: You never know who might show up, and over the years we had a few pleasant and not so pleasant surprises.

Europeans are quite adept at calling up at the last minute and saying, I'm in the neighborhood, can I drop by and "see your office," "say hello," "talk to you about a business situation." Quite a few times I recall hearing, "So-and-So from country X or State Y is outside and wants to know if you are free to say hello for a minute." (One thing about New York, people do pass through all the time.) I could not say no to some of these people, and was in fact quite happy to see many of them. When they met with me in my office, I was Clicquot, Inc., and Veuve Clicquot. I was the face and image of the brand. You don't have to be the CEO for that. Every manager of any kind gets these cold-call visits from friends and business associates, and in those moments, they are their company and their brands. So, don't take clothing risks.

I am not a *fashionista*, yet, like most French women, I do love nice clothes, I do feel upbeat and prepared to face the world when I feel I look chic, and, like all of us, I enjoy being complimented on my choices (if you don't like or get compliments on your appearance, maybe it is a signal). Since we are all unique, different both in shape and taste, it's up to each of us to develop a personal style. That's being your own brand. Consider these (universal) basics and accent them for yourself. You don't have to agree with me, but you should know why you do not . . . then sleep on your decision.

1. Dress smexy (smart and sexy, and by sexy I mean feminine and fashionable but, again, not anything that reveals too much—that, in my vocabulary, is totally not sexy). Mother's advice for business and life keeps coming back: Never show too much. Let them (men) use their imagination. . . . Keep a little mystery.

2. Invest in "good staples," i.e., quality over quantity, for your core collection.

3. No one has a perfect body, so the trick is to put an accent on the positive and camouflage the rest. I'll humbly say that the typical French woman is usually good at this.

4. Learn to stay within the boundaries of your personal style, especially for a special occasion (i.e., don't go wild at sunset and wear an atypically revealing dress; that creates mixed messages and misunderstandings about you in business settings and beyond).

That Fashion, Femininity, and Fun (FFF) go together is something one discovers over a lifetime, and like anything in life, its expression changes through various stages of life. But it should give pleasures, lots of small ones. The trick is not to confuse glamour with girliness. Also, avoid the "total look" or "it must match" attitude, which is so anti-French. As you may have heard, if one notices that a woman is too put together—i.e., pink outfit with matching shoes and bag . . . headband, even hat, jewelry, *ad nauseam*—she probably is not. It speaks for her brand, though. What a brand. Opt for the understated elegance that is not noticeable but is there. Call it Chic Simplicity . . . or understated elegance.

To conclude this little discourse on clothes, here is my take on some specific basics to get you started. Then it's up to you to create your style and mix and match (rather than *coordinate*, a word overused by retailer staff to make you buy more!), always keeping a "comfort first" (though not synonymous with "casual") attitude (there's no point walking in stilettos if you can't walk without twisting your ankles, a funny sight on NYC sidewalks).

A conventional, basic "never go out of style" business wardrobe that you can build around in your quest for personal image and style includes these classics. I call it the IPT or Indispensable Pulled Together wardrobe that will get you far:

- A little black dress—okay, I may appear repetitive on this one, but it is *obligatoire* (sleeveless and A-line work best for most of us).

- A cashmere cardigan in a neutral color.

- A crewneck sweater contrasting with the cardigan.

- A black turtleneck.

- A white blouse with high collar (great for interviews—a collar equals authority, self-confidence), a
V-neck or classic camisole, and a cotton T-shirt.

- A pair of quality pumps, a pair of stilettos, a pair of
loafers or comfortable walking shoes, and the ubiqui-
tous "ballerina" flats, as well as sandals for vacation.
Boots optional. Recreational shoes don't count for
business. And if four or five pairs of shoes are not in
your current budget or not what you consider basic for
business, then buy two good pairs for work. Over time
it seems the quantity takes care of itself, yet noticeably
cheap quality always looks cheap. And remember,
shoes are one of the "tells" in a first impression.

- A tailored (i.e., well-cut/cropped) jacket. Avoid long
or double-breasted jackets, which make most of us
look dumpy. Pick some bright color (but not too
bright) to contrast with dark pants.

- Well-cut pants—neither too baggy nor too tight—in
black, navy, gray, or tan.

- A formal but feminine suit with either pencil skirt or
straight or slightly flared pants. Tip: Nonpleated
pants give you a taller, thinner look.

- A cocktail dress (avoid big prints, horizontal stripes,
or flowers unless you plan to be in Hawaii).

- A casual outfit for traveling.

- A few silk scarves and a pashmina or cashmere wrap (for evenings and/or planes).

- A classic raincoat and/or winter coat that can be worn with or without belt.

- A couple of small and long necklaces: Keep the short ones for suits, jackets, and V-neck tops, and wear the long ones over dresses and tunics. Remember that a pearl necklace is the dream accessory that is timeless. Think mood, too: calm goes with small, energy with big. . . . Jewelry tells a lot about our unique personality. And don't be afraid to mix precious with costume jewelry.

- A practical and pretty (trendy, chic in soft leather) handbag (no stuffed supersize, please, as it destroys your overall look). I love the lightweight bags. I adopt the 50 percent solution for the bigger bag and encourage you to visit the contents of your bag periodically and get rid of the nonessential . . . usually 50 percent. Tip: When you buy a bag, if it weighs three to five pounds empty—and you'll be surprised how many do—skip it. (I remember one young woman who, while searching for a pen, dropped two-thirds of her bag's contents on the floor, and it amused me to see the makeup items mixed with tea bags, cigarettes, tampons, and costume jewelry good for a strip bar visit, among many other "indispensable" items.)

Optional: a chic wallet, an interesting watch, a striking belt, and a great pair (*peut-être deux*) of sunglasses that frame your face well.

Remember that your clothes are your ambassadors, whether formal or casual. And, again, don't forget the smile, your ultimate accessory. It's always in season.

French women tend to justify their clothes shopping splurges on a pay-per-wear basis and prefer the 33 euros for 100 compliments exchange to the 100 euros for 33 compliments. After all, anyone can get a compliment on a $10,000 couture gown!

At a presentation I was making in Shanghai, a young and gorgeous Chinese woman in the audience wanted to know the designer of my "couture outfit." (I get this question more than one might guess!) I was pleased to describe the Belgian jacket, American sweater, Italian pants, and shoes from small, unknown designers, as well as the French underwear of quality though with no couture name attached to them (in any case, I cut off the labels . . . who needs them?). I'm not sure it was an epiphany or a revelation, but I suspect she and other Chinese women in the audience learned that French women are very individualistic in the way they dress, and I'm happy to see the trend in other countries.

....

ARTIFICIAL "SWEETENERS"

The scent of a woman—a phrase borrowed from the title of an Academy Award–winning film—is the signifier of a unique identity. Our scents and smells set us apart from all others. "I love your smell" certainly has been uttered romantically countless times in many languages through the centuries.

In our world, reawakened to aromatherapy, the power of some scents to calm or excite is being championed. The power of our own natural scents and odors, transpiring to varying degrees through our singular bodies and pores, has long had the power of sexual attraction or repulsion. Today, a host of synthetic products, from hair products to skin creams and soaps, give us scent identities, often unwittingly. What messages is your scent sending about you? It is part of your packaging.

We can control our aroma and use it as part of our brand identity, of course, especially through the soap we use and the perfume we wear. Perfume has existed for at least four thousand years that we know of, and has been popular among aristocrats since the Renaissance and with the rest of us starting in the eighteenth century. We no longer have to put perfumed handkerchiefs to our noses as we pass through foul-smelling streets, and in our twenty-first-century developed world, now that weekly baths are a forgotten ritual of our ancestors, we generally don't need more scent to disguise body odors; perfume is a discretionary accessory, to be managed to our advantage and protected from becoming a disadvantage.

I am not a fan of strong perfumes. In business, the scent of a strong perfume can mean disaster at a job interview or a dinner party with fine wine and foods. (You'll certainly be noticed and distinguished from others.) All you really need is a light, fresh scent for the warm months and perhaps a spicy or musky one for the cold months. I am faithful to one scent.

The perfume industry is huge and unbelievably competitive, as anyone who has walked the main floor of a department store and been assaulted by smells, mists, and hawkers knows. It is in a bit of a decline, though, as price is a barrier for many and promotion is exceedingly expensive. Quality costs, too. The finest and most consistent blends are made from extracts and essential oils of costly natural ingredients. The industry plays more and more with synthetic engineered scents, and many new perfumes are front-loaded with bursting, compelling sweet flavors that lead to a quick sale but wear off relatively rapidly, revealing more neutral and thin composition (and perhaps to a bottle unused on a shelf at home). A nod to price is the availability of a brand's *eau de parfum* or *eau de toilette*, diluted and shorter-lived concentrations of aromatic compounds but still the real thing. And here's another money-saving secret: Buy the smallest bottle. Perfume, like wine, oxidizes, especially in a bottle half full (or less). And if you're using perfume sparingly, the bottle will oxidize and lose its magic before you can ever reach the bottom.

My mother's perfume is my perfume, Chanel No. 5, the celebrated jasmine- and rose-infused fragrance chosen by Coco Chanel in 1921. Chanel said, "A woman should wear fragrance wherever she expects to be kissed." My mother's gift of my first bottle of perfume was an important rite of passage to woman-hood. But as far as quotes go, I prefer Marilyn Monroe's endorsement of my perfume. When asked what she wore in bed, she purred, "Two drops of Chanel No. 5." How's that for exclamation points attached to a signature? For me, one drop of exclamation point works just fine, thank you.

....

MANNERS

The manners you wear are another kind of perfume, and manners play a larger than usually recognized role in defining one's style and brand. Etiquette—as in business etiquette—is perhaps a more apt word for socially acceptable, even expected, behaviors.

Over time and history, we collectively agreed to spell cat with a *c* and not a *k* so we can communicate in writing with each other, whether English is our first or fifth language, whether we live in England or Ecuador. We learn conventional business practices and culture so we can be effective on the job and send a signal that we are trained and professional.

If there's an area where role models and mentoring are important, it is in sharing the many unwritten as well as written rules of conduct that make the people part of the business equation work. Remember thank-you correspondence? What about being on time for meetings? In our global economy, awareness of how business etiquette depends on culture is part of being a professional, so that what works in one city or country might not only not work in another but may kill a deal by creating a poor impression or even insulting a host or business associate. It is one thing not to appreciate that business cards in China and the Far East are presented with two hands and a little bow of the head. It is another thing and not a good one in the Persian Gulf to cross your legs and show the soles of your feet or shoes to a potential person of influence or sovereign business leader.

How you embrace and demonstrate manners or etiquette sets you apart. Your special touches further define your brand. Dealing with tragedy in a colleague's life I found to be a tricky but defining moment. It can be a statement of character as well as style, and also a revealing two-way communication. Your approach to offering anything, from condolences to statements of support, has to be subtle and understated if it is going to be well received by the person to whom it is directed. But such an approach is not always understood by others on the outside, who may not fully grasp your relationship with the person. I had my share of that—to cite an extreme example—dealing with the effects of 9/11 on different members of my staff in New York, all of whom were touched in close, personal ways, and some of whom required individual outreach. During the course of business life such moments of individual loss or grief are inevitable and cannot be ignored; they call for a special class of decorum and acquired savoir faire.

In all my years of business, I never used profanity. I did not set out to do that and I'm not a prude—I've certainly heard enough of it—but I was sensitive early in my career to my audience; some found it vulgar or were indeed offended by it coming from a woman, so I never used it. Over the years I never found the need for it in order to be effective. Similarly, I never found the need to raise my voice, which surely distinguished me, especially as shouting and profanity became more and more commonplace and tolerated (if not accepted) in the white-collar workplace. One can be firm with a smile and persuasive without screaming (anger is often the weapon of a weak person). Always understand and respect your audience.

Etiquette and standards are regularly evolving, of course, and I confess to having wanted to shout a few times via email, but, of course, one of the earliest lessons we learn is not to hit the send key when we are angry or upset. And not to shout by typing in all caps. (Did someone teach you that or did you have to learn those two lessons, as I did, by trial and error?) There's also merit in the oft offered and rarely followed advice of not putting anything in an email you would not say to someone's face (this includes your boss's). Many people have learned this the hard way: Your written words, even via email, are safest when they are identical to how you conduct yourself in person. And haven't we all experienced a wider audience for our electronic communications than we anticipated *à la* "cc" and "forward" buttons? An entire "netiquette" has emerged for communicating using technologies. Most people understand that flame wars are to be avoided, though, sadly, spreading gossip or false or misleading information, often anonymously, over the net seems to be a sport for some.

Business etiquette is acquired through experience and certainly extends to business dining and entertaining, where around a table there are many accepted and expected practices that may sometimes seem as arbitrary as whether we spell cat with *c* or *k*.

Take the use of the napkin in restaurants. Recently I took a well-educated European woman in her late twenties to a top restaurant and came to realize that she did not know to open the folded napkin and put it on her lap. Surprising but no crime. She did not come from a family that could afford dining out while she was growing up, nor could she afford it now. She simply lacked experience at so-called white tablecloth restaurants, which are standard in the business world. I suspect that at home she and her family kept the napkin on the table, and perhaps it was always paper and not cloth.

I cite this story to show again how manners distinguish a person . . . and to ask a business etiquette question. Say you are at a business dinner and halfway through the meal you have to get up—an urgent call of nature or phone call—what do you do with your napkin? I've seen people take it with them, but most put it on or alongside their plate. It is a petty detail, really, but the keepers of the code say you should place it on your chair. If you knew the finer points of etiquette and that answer, you would notice when someone placed their napkin on the table, so what would you think? That it doesn't matter? Remember why we spell cat with a *c*? For one thing, you'd be noticed and look uneducated if you spelled it with a *k*. What if someone poured red wine into a white-wine glass? Also minor and arbitrary, but noticeable and telling to those in the know. It is like someone ending the salutation of a business letter with a comma rather than a colon. Not knowing the locally accepted etiquette can diminish you in the eyes of others. Knowing it is safer and distinguishing. We all make *faux pas*—no cause for depression or defensiveness—learn from those around you and move ahead. Etiquette evolves, but it helps to know the current practices in whatever circles you are attempting to conduct business.

Netiquette extends to the dining table as well and varies among cultures. In my world, smartphones should be turned off during business and other meals or, if turned to vibrate, left un-answered/unread during the meal. I don't appreciate hearing other people's inane phone conversations, virtually all of which could either wait or never need to happen at all. In the Persian Gulf, however, it is seemingly impolite not to answer your smartphone, and during business meetings or dinners such inter-ruptions are expected. Is answering your phone or texting in the company of others part of your brand? Doing so makes a state-ment about you and your style and manners.

One thing about those cozy, romantic Parisian bistros, they squeeze the tables in, and with six inches on either side of your table, your inadvertent dining companions for the evening are your immediate neighbors to your right and left. And this situa-tion is not restricted to Paris or to bistros. Edward and I recently found ourselves in a trendy new Paris retro bistro next to an American couple in their early thirties, and despite our attempts not to listen to their conversation, we gleaned they were recently engaged. They were whispering to one another, sharing food, and clearly delighted with the food and experience. Just after they finished their meals, on some silent command they both whipped out their smartphones and for a good five minutes sat in the middle of the restaurant with screens twelve inches from their eyes, reading, texting, and emailing away with intense concentration and frozen faces from faraway places.

At least they were not *talking* on their phones so that everyone would hear variations on "the cheese course was delicious," but we still wondered whether this is an inevitable shift in social grace to the acceptance of present-tense community sharing. We hope not. It points to an inability to live in and savor the moment unless it is externally recorded . . . abstracting and distancing it. It also signals a selfish indulgence and disregard for the diners at your elbows or elsewhere in the room. Okay, photographs freeze a moment in time, and perhaps a quick flashless photo of a couple or mostly of what is on the plate in a good restaurant is here with us to stay, but how much of the future or external world must we accept without distorting the here and now?

. . . .

TRAINING

Being your own brand requires work and training. If you work for a luxury goods company you are a walking advertisement for the brand, which means you have to "live" the brand to some extent. In the Champagne and fine wine sector, you'll need to know your way around wine service and dining and related etiquettes. Over the years I increasingly witnessed a lack of table manners among our new and growing staff (and I don't mean where they placed their napkin when they left the table— more like starting to eat before everyone was served) and decided that a diplomatic way to address it was to incorporate a little "etiquette" session in our national sales meeting. It worked well, saved me numerous embarrassments, set a style, and more often than not made a favorable impression upon the guests we were entertaining. The training was about who sits where at a table, who orders, who tastes the wine, and how. Moreover, it was about all the glasses one faced in front of the plates and the silverware on each side of them; yes, the napkin; and the art of conversation. In some other industries, this kind of training might not be as important, but to some it is invaluable.

One year, our chairman from France attended the sales meeting and was simply shocked at that particular training session. (Of course, he never ran a staff training for a restaurant or hotel staff or presented a Champagne tasting to people who had never tried Champagne.) He came from a time and place where you learned all of this at your family's Sunday dinner (that is, lunch). "Are your staff barbarians that they don't know that? In France, it would be laughed at," he said, and I remember his exact choice of words well . . . and my reply. "Well, don't be so sure." A few years later, with the rapid growth of our group and having embraced a philosophy of mobility, several perfect young French men from sister companies and business sectors landed in New York as part of our team. Guess what? I would not call them barbarians, but they surely were not acculturated to subtleties of fine wine, food, service, and the overall professional deportment consistent with our luxury image and brands.

One night, with the chairman present, we witnessed innocent but embarrassingly gauche behaviors by "high-potential" employees that confirmed my belief in lifelong education of a lifestyle kind. You've seen the kind of guy who chews like a cow, talks with his mouth open, and stains the white tablecloth around his plate with polka dots. Before I knew it, my message, philosophy, and approach were discussed and embraced at a very high level at LVMH in Paris, and etiquette and "how to dress" sessions were developed in less than a year and became mandatory in France for all management personal. Simply a sign of the times. It started at the top in a classic trickle-down approach, then was extended to the rest of the international divisions and their armies of employees. Forty to fifty lucky ones at a time got a free trip to France to attend the sessions and learn about internationalism, cultural differences, dress codes, and eating rituals. Admittedly, some gentlemen (and women) felt insulted, but going through a "quiz" before the course, it was clear they all could learn a thing or two about table manners and dress code.

Now, the LVMH group being a large one, a whole crew of outside people was hired to put together a long and elaborate doctrine (with accompanying practice, where men learn how to tie their ties properly, for example) and incorporate it into staff training worldwide. In slow economic times it might be given a rest for a few years, but I suspect it is here to stay. At the end of the day, it's now understood that you are what (and how) you eat (and drink), and you are how you dress. In the luxury world, first impressions and basic good manners are an art that can no longer be neglected. It's part of the show. It matters. Actually, in all business sectors, style and manners of the appropriate kind make *la différence*.

WHOSE SUCCESS?

I do not like the word *success*, never have. I rarely use it, so it is perhaps ironic that it appears in this chapter's title. It is a relative term; one person's "success" would be a disappointment or even a failure to another. And, looking back on life, just how important are little business "successes"? I always feel foolish and a bit self-conscious using the word. I do not want to think or feel that I am taking myself and business too seriously. People care about success, though, and want it. But what is it?

Success is about managing expectations—your expectations and likely those of the people closest to you. How many children are told by their parents and grandparents that they are gorgeous or smart or brilliant and they should grow up to be a doctor, lawyer, or Indian chief? (Or similar unachievables for most. By the way, are there any female Indian chiefs?) And we know that often what they are projecting for others is what *they* want for us, and really perhaps what they had wished for themselves, not what *we* want. But we understand they do want the best for us, and we try to and perhaps do forgive them, though for many the psychological trauma of failing to meet the expectations of loved ones is costly.

For women, the longest-standing expectation for success is to have babies—grandchildren and, in many cultures throughout history, specifically male heirs. In the twenty-first century, how is that "personal" expectation reconciled with career success and happiness? Many women want it all, but I believe that is not possible, unless you manage your expectations of what "having it all" means. Surely it is possible to have a happy marriage, a couple of kids, and a decent career. Not easy, but possible. It is the rare, remarkable woman, however, who can be an astronaut, a nurturing wife, and the readily available mother of four or five. (Does she exist?) And while I am tempted to say that in some contemporary, urban, and developed societies today, children are not a standard of success for many women, worldwide I suspect I'd be on shaky ground.

Setting and managing our own expectations defines success and a path to balance and happiness. My advice is, don't get too caught up in long-term definitions; chew on manageable short-term goals and benchmarks or you will only get frustrated, depressed, or worse. I'll never be a great pianist (oh, happy day, when they invented electric pianos with earphones), so my consuming goal is to learn a new, simple piece—a great pleasure and reward I appreciate fully when achieved. Thinking bigger might just keep me away from the simple pleasure of playing. If you want to speak another language, a month or two of study will not get you there. Be realistic. Set up a goal of completing a level-one course, or five chapters in a book. Once you've achieved that, pat yourself on the back and set your next target goals. Ditto for a career. Focus on the job you have and the next one you want, not the ultimate one you want. And remember balance and life.

If you are the kind of person who worries or worried in your twenties about how much you should be investing for your retirement, you need to think harder about living your life in phases and resetting your measures for success along the way.

We are challenged today in our consumer-oriented, instant-gratification world by external benchmarks thrust at us. On Wall Street people keep score by income, bonuses, and net worth. The best-selling issue of *Forbes* each year is the one with the ranking of the world's billionaires. Others keep score by the size of their home. A lot of people keep score by job title and responsibility.

In *French Women for All Seasons*, I remarked *en passant* how French people generally do not introduce or define people by what they do for a living, while Americans routinely do. "I'd like you to meet Jill, she's an accountant for Boeing." I prefer saying, "I'd like you to meet Jill, she's just back from Mexico." In New York, I know how I am introduced at parties, and it can be awkward hearing about myself and makes me think about how some of the other women in the room feel about me. Not so in France. In Paris recently, Edward and I had dinner at a restaurant with new friends, an American-born woman who has lived in France for twenty years, and her French husband, whom we were meeting for the first time. We had a lovely time, and after two and a half hours left not knowing his profession at all. It was reassuring. Isn't defining ourselves and others by our job titles reductive and boring?

Clothes and brands are another way people keep score. Why else would we see all those real and fake Louis Vuitton monogrammed bags? As I've shared before, I am so frequently asked what brand of clothes or what "designer" I am wearing, I am no longer surprised by it. How you dress certainly makes important and powerful nonverbal statements about you, but also reveals how and what others consider success and how it is conveyed.

In the business of life, one must consider one's definitions of success for the long term and the short term, and revisit these thoughts periodically. As in any plan, there will be trade-offs and compromises—wealth versus altruism, passion versus talent, work versus vacation, family versus career, and so on. What is perfectly clear about life and business plans is that they have a relatively short shelf life. It might be nice at twenty to think about what a successful life might be when fifty, but at best it is only a far, distant star by which to navigate. It is much more realistic to fix a short-term definition and plan. Graduating from college is perhaps the most common and sound career decision and measure of success for a twenty-one-year-old, the necessary antecedent to the next phase in life and reconsideration of success. Besides, who knows what the career options will be in thirty years? Thirty years ago, careers in Detroit's auto industry were still a big thing and dot-com jobs were nonexistent.

A woman's life expectancy in many developed nations now stretches well into the eighties and, with advances in science and medicine, has the potential to increase significantly beyond that. The perspective with which a twenty-, thirty-, or forty-year-old today looks upon life and success is far removed from that of our grandmothers, who when young probably thought everyone retired by sixty-five and would probably be dead by seventy-five. (In France, people angle to retire on government pensions at fifty-five or as early as possible, although that is changing, too.)

When I was in my twenties, had moved to New York, and had figured out that I no longer wanted to be a translator-interpreter but not much more in terms of "career" (a word woman even then did not commonly use), I decided to teach a few French courses at the Alliance Française. Partly I wanted to see if I liked teaching French, partly I needed to align my work schedule with my new husband's, a university professor (read June, July, and August off), and partly I hoped to stay in touch with and wave the flag of France, which I was missing a bit. Yes, I was young. One of my students, Doug, was an impressive corporate attorney, probably in his early forties, who lived in Westchester. His French wasn't half bad, but he had never been to France. It was his dream, though at the time he seemingly lived the American dream of a good job, a wife, two kids, two cars, and a house in a wealthy suburb of New York City. No doubt he had a hefty mortgage and car loans as well. What he did not have were the sort of life experiences I assumed such a smart guy would have and could afford. He had traveled outside the States once, as

I recall . . . but not even on a London, Paris, or Rome introductory tour. This shocked me. He wanted to travel but was on some sort of life plan that included sending kids to college but would not include living much of the life he wanted for another decade, if ever. He seemed trapped and was consuming life mindlessly.

Okay, perhaps I exaggerate—and I admire that he set himself a personal goal and pleasure in learning French and was achieving it—but I thought then and think now that there has to be a powerful element of living life in the present in any balanced personal definition of success. That I was able to take some multimonth travel vacations in my twenties is one of the most gratifying pleasures of my life. With my passion for fine food, being the youngest person in a Michelin three-star restaurant was a kick for me, though it might not be for everyone. I did not want to wait, like Doug, till I was forty or fifty, or forever. The experiences I seized were transformational, informing my ideas and conversation to this day and confirming a personal passion for travel and culture that directly influenced my career and life choices.

I was balancing the present against the future. In the world today, when forty is the new thirty, or in nip-and-tuck Beverly Hills, where people say sixty is the new forty (though I am not sure the body inside always agrees, and there are days when fifty-nine is the new sixty), it is not shocking to recognize that in America, adolescence really ends at thirty. You do not have to have Doug's house in the country, a dog, two kids, and a decent job by thirty to be a success. You are forgiven. You can get married and divorced. You are forgiven. You can go back to school, stop out of school, take a job, quit a job, change careers. You are forgiven. It is the time to take some risks, experiment and experience, because the consequences are not severe and things generally work out. You have time at thirty and forty to recover and start new and satisfying stages of life.

Now, if being a brain surgeon is part of your personal definition for success, or if you want to earn millions by the age of thirty, then you'll have to put off some of those vacations, four-hour restaurant experiences, and other leisure pleasures for some years. But we are *not* what we do for a living. To me and to many others, actor or waiter, artist or banker, you are either an interesting, nice person or not. I do, though, recommend getting your entry-level degrees, as in B.A., M.A., M.B.A., or possibly J.D. out of the way during "adolescence." And for those careers that require the M.D. or Ph.D. as a starting credential? You can probably rule out adolescence, but not by much.

Here's what some leading women in business were doing at age thirty: Martha Stewart, ex-model, married and mother of one daughter, was a stockbroker; Meg Whitman had followed her new husband to San Francisco and worked at the consulting firm Bain & Company; Suze Orman, financial guru, author, and cable TV host, was just out of a seven-year waitressing career at Buttercup Bakery in Berkeley, California; Hillary Clinton was a junior attorney at the Rose Law Firm in Little Rock, Arkansas; Oprah Winfrey moved to Chicago to host MLS-TV's morning talk show, *AM Chicago*. As for me, I was not on any successful career path at thirty that I recognized. I was an inexperienced account executive in a small New York City PR firm, working for the Champagne industry. And I was happy as far as I understood happiness.

We mostly know when we are happy (sometimes in retrospect) and what makes us happy, and we know from social psychologists that it does not correlate with wealth beyond reaching a "comfortable" level. What's financially comfortable? We must define it ourselves . . . ability to put food on the table and perhaps have enough left over to drink wine with it? What wine? We may aspire for great wealth or great wines and think it is part of our happiness formula, but of course it is not. And our definition of success will change with our phases in life. Guys buy a Porsche and think they are successful and happy or whatever (sexy?). Eventually they give up those cars. Women buy what? Jewelry? Handbags? And that makes them successful and happy?

Being comfortable with ourselves is a better indicator of "success" than the handbag we carry, but that bag or our ability to own it is often tied to our self-actualization and identity. Therein lies the recurrent challenge of managing our expectations and psychological head games. One thing I know, mediocrity is the enemy of success, and we should not fool ourselves into thinking good is great.

I was recently reminded of this in an offbeat way. The trigger was a week spent in northern Italy. Each day the coffee was ambrosial. Rich, strong, flavorful, creamy espresso. When I returned home to my usual pod-based, machine-generated consistent espresso—better than most and pleasing, I had convinced myself—I thought, who am I kidding? After the shocking reminder of great coffee in Italy, I realized that I had become conditioned to good, not great, and that I was cheating myself. We cannot procure greatness or success in everything we buy or produce, but knowing the true merits of what we touch is important in establishing our personal standards and setting ourselves apart in a few areas. Most important perhaps, it keeps us from mindless mediocrity.

Feeling *bien dans sa peau* (comfortable in one's skin) is an attitude that changes with your decades and is more in your head than in fact. Define short-term success for yourself—success is, after all, fundamentally subjective—and if you need to lose thirty pounds, set an immediate goal of five. Bite-size portions work.

....

MANAGE THE METRICS

I began this chapter by pointing out that success is about managing expectations, mostly your own. However, an essential and common theme in a successful career in business is managing your performance to your company's or boss's expectations and managing your company's or boss's expectations of you. Warning 1: Do not promise too much. Warning 2: Do not promise too little. Recommendation: Learn to identify and commit to aggressive but realistically achievable goals. Definition of success in business: meeting or exceeding your goals. Period. End of story.

In practice that could mean something as simple as saying no to the boss who asks for the report on Friday when you know

....

that regardless of how much effort you put into it, you cannot get it done well before the following Tuesday. In practice, that could mean not volunteering to deliver a report on Friday when you are not certain you can (and we all underestimate time, as a result of which you'll spend your weekend working).

Being able to forecast accurately and deliver quality earns respect, even if it involves a little pushback.

Performance evaluations are about measuring performance against goals, and it is safest to keep the measures as objective as possible. For a woman that can be a protection against a double standard. That also means going into a performance period with a clear set of objectives and agreed-upon outcomes that would signify achievement of those goals. Unless you are employed as an investment counselor or in a similar occupation where the rate of return pretty much says it all about your performance, there's always a degree of subjectivity in evaluations . . . a so-called fudge factor, such as say, your leadership performance or communications skills or team play. I always used them to round up or down, especially at bonus time.

There is a temptation to tell your boss what she wants to hear. "Double sales? Okay." Avoid that sort of behavior: It can be dangerous for you if you have not properly assessed whether the goal is within your ability to deliver it. And some bosses and companies are predictable in their push of very aggressive goals on people, even while most know what is reasonable and always know what is modest. I routinely gave people stretch goals individually and was transparent about the fact that the sum of everyone's goals exceeded the company's and my individual goals.

I certainly was not going to let someone work toward anything lower than a top performance mark, and I was not going to let one or a few individuals prevent the company from hitting our numbers, hurting all of us. So I built in a cushion.

Equally important, agreeing on performance goals protects you from getting the rules of the game changed on you late in the day. That is, if you are exceeding agreed-upon expectations, don't let the boss raise the bar on you, at least without new negotiations. You may find your numbers just getting bigger and bigger but you'll never be regarded as "successful" in that period.

For myself and for my company, I always forecast and promised aggressive but achievable outcomes. And I always exceeded them, and that was a key to my "success" in business. It did not just happen: It took smart work, hard work, focus, constant re-evaluation, and sometimes fresh and aggressive new "restorative" interventions and plans, timely actions often months before others saw a challenge, and, of course, a great team capable of executing our plans fully. If I had unrealistically promised more and just missed it, I'd be telling a different tale. Or, to paraphrase Dickens, promise a 20 percent increase, deliver a 19 percent increase, result—unhappiness even unemployment. Promise a 20 percent increase, deliver a 21 percent increase, result—happiness and a raise.

Outperforming market benchmarks and exceeding your goals allows you to keep your job and perhaps pop a few corks of Champagne.

7

FIRE YOUR BOSS:
LEADERS AND MANAGERS

R emember that classic dilemma and all-important decision I had to make that would change my life? The job, the man, the city, the country? The man or the job . . . the job or the man?

That's when my mother taught me a prime management principle, and it is a wonder to me how she came to embrace it in the first place, living a simple life in rural France of another era: Don't let fear be a barrier to achieving your ambitions or seizing opportunities.

At those times of opportunity, risk, and decision, she taught me to ask myself, *What's the worst thing that can happen?* It has become my mantra and always served me well.

When I was conflicted over the choice to move to America—a decision that was certainly painful for my mother—she indeed asked me, "What's the worst thing that could happen? . . . You come back," she answered, "and we'll be here for you." What was the worst that could happen, I asked myself, if I quit my good job and gambled on Champagne Veuve Clicquot? I'd be on the job market in another year or two? Not so risky after all. Not a month goes by when I don't have occasion to think of my mother's advice and ask myself her question. It has made all the difference.

One of the characteristics of a good leader is a calculated lack of fear that translates into making tough and even risky decisions and inspiring confidence. I learned from my mother that it can be an acquired trait.

To begin with a basic business truth, successful companies—and no doubt families—have good leaders and good managers (well, almost always). Recognizing that leadership and management are discrete talents and skill sets and that they are not distributed equally in individuals begins to delineate organization charts and career paths as well as useful self-realization. "Management is doing things right; leadership is doing the right things," is a memorable differentiator coined by famed business writer and educator Peter Drucker.

Warren Buffett, the renowned Berkshire Hathaway chairman, regularly cited over the past decade as the world's richest man, has made a large fortune investing in companies with good management. Lots of merchant bankers and investment funds have made or lost large sums investing in companies with poor management, then bringing in new managers. But there are leaders and there are leaders, and there are managers as well as managers, of course. A "turnaround" artist has the experience and skills to lead a quick makeover, but probably not to nurture a brand or company over the long term. Small companies require a certain type of leader, large companies another. The smaller the company, the more likely the leadership and the key management roles are combined; the larger the company, the less likely. Leading and managing a mature company requires people with different skill sets than a start-up, perhaps even starting with such a nonskill as having sufficient gray hairs to invite respect and project a "beard" of wisdom. And companies are dynamic, so a set of good leaders and managers in today's context may not be so in tomorrow's context.

I do not have the spirit of a CEO of a billion-dollar corporation, so, as my firm consistently grew in digits and I found myself at more and more meetings and further and further from our customers as well as my employees, I knew a new stage was dawning. Besides, the CEO can be at least 40 percent of the face of a company, and while wrinkles work well for men representing venerable companies, it still seems less the case for women and spokespersons. The luxury goods business is, ironically, about youth and romance, even though the majority of the people who can afford luxury items are not young. People desire and buy the best in its prime, even if it is to recapture memories. A mature and "rounder" Catherine Deneuve may appear in a highly retouched Louis Vuitton ad, but she is selling and representing—it seems to me—her iconic image of youth, beauty, sex, and sophistication. People, young and old, don't want to be the current vintage of Catherine, they want to be her in the best vintage (though many will take her in any rendition).

While leadership is multifaceted, contextual, transient, there is no escaping that extraordinary leadership makes all the difference in a company. Being a business leader is not quite the same thing as being a political leader, but permit me to use an illustration from government. (Ironically, we routinely trust the running of our government business to people who often have little top business leadership experience.) I have lived through a host of New York City mayors, some of them quite nice and seemingly able, but the consensus for their performance was that New York City was just too big and complex to govern and was subject to far too much outside government control or influence. And then came Rudy Giuliani (no, I am not now nor have I ever been his wife, though I am often asked, especially when I hand over my credit card) and next Mike Bloomberg. Wow, what a difference. Crime, labor, schools, finance, optimism—all decisively better. Timing is one thing, chance another, but good leaders at the right time exploit opportunities and bring transformational change.

Whether you are already a leader, aspiring to be one, or perhaps even hiring one, it is important to one's business life and success to recognize good leadership. What follows is my take on some telltale characteristics, plus some observations on my own leadership style, and finally, some observations on good general operational elements of management.

How do you recognize an outstanding leader and hook your star to theirs, which I recommend as a surefire get-ahead approach? You should pick your bosses and know your boss's boss carefully—and "fire" the bad ones quickly by getting yourself into a new situation. Spot early the true leaders, who will take your company or another firm to good places, and the talented managers who will be there for the ride. Being part of their team is acting in one's enlightened self-interest. So, what are the telltale characteristics of a good leader?

- Great communication skills. In part, that is what got Barack Obama elected as president. Who would have thought that history would rate Ronald Reagan the finest American president over the past fifty years and more? President Reagan was known as the "great communicator." The former actor could tell a story. He looked into the camera and looked into your eyes and spoke to you believably. He was clear, direct, and persuasive. He could be funny, smiled a lot, and was inspirational to many. He was the master of oral communication, through television, radio, public speeches, and small group meetings. But outstanding leaders do not have to be actors or TV personalities to reach their constituents. People follow leaders who communicate their ideas effectively and can motivate people emotionally and logically, meeting their eyes, voice, heart, or prose whether in person or electronically.

  Today's leaders also have to navigate a changing digital landscape that has made communications access to and from a leader and leadership team only an email away.

- Good leaders do not complicate things; they simplify them by identifying and repeating key ideas and a vision into which they fit. Good leaders help keep the charge clear and simple. Sometimes leaders create a vision for a company; other times they inherit one, but they align strategy, values, and funding toward achieving that vision and make management and staff believers in their vision and strategy. They eliminate confusion.

Our annual corporate retreat held in late January or early February with dozens of people coming in from all over the country was a highly effective management tool, helping to clarify and simplify our actions and getting everyone on board with our vision and plan. Reviewing the previous year's strong results and the particular sales and marketing actions that worked especially well not only helped to endorse the company vision but, by sharing the successes, also bonded people who saw their individual contributions tied to the overall good of the company and motivated them for greater success. Repeating the company's core values and messages in various presentations ensured that everyone was on the same page and could talk the talk. Part refresher course, part update on our company's and each of our brands' DNA and sales and marketing plans, the program reduced, repeated, and clarified essential takeaway knowledge via presentations and question-and-answer discussions. All of this preceded the presentation of the company's goals for the year and then the fixing of each individual's personal goals (that part was done in private). Everyone left the meeting knowing the three to five major company objectives for the year and the three to five individual goals that they had to meet *and* how they fit into the whole for the company to have a good year.

What I've just described is a clear, simple, transparent, unifying, motivating, and team-building event when done properly . . . and it was my job each year as the company leader not to run or manage the meeting but to ensure that it was focused and done properly; to deliver the clarion messages on vision, values, and strategy; and to sum up with clarity the prime issues for the coming year.

- Success builds success, and consistently being fair and effective builds loyalty: A good leader always builds loyalty and takes care of her people. Aren't we loyal to a person who has shown that she understands our needs and who acknowledges and rewards our efforts? And I don't mean through instant gratification, but over time and when the need or right opportunity presents itself.

- Good leaders also do not try to manage many things or people or micromanage but surround themselves with talented managers and let them do their jobs. That's commonplace gospel in theory, rarer in execution.

- Indecisiveness is not a trait of a good leader, obviously. People want someone who can make the tough decisions and make them clearly. Effective leaders have thick skins, so they can avoid the pressure for quick decisions and manage the timing of decisions for the greater good of the company, and they can make unpopular decisions. People seek and respect firm leadership.

- Consistency is a valuable trait in an effective leader. People don't like surprises in business, and there's comfort in knowing the reaction of the boss in advance; it shapes how people act and informs a culture. Even if the boss has some questionable proclivities—say, being a bully over some ideas or people, which Rudy Giuliani was accused of—people recognize it and deal with it in context: "Rudy's just being Rudy." It goes with the package. One can reject the package, of course, as voters often do. As an employee, you can always vote with your feet on the election day of your choice.

- Effective leaders possess a self-confidence that is contagious. And they are not afraid to hire highly talented people. They are not threatened by them. Who doesn't want to believe in their boss and their boss's ability to do what they say and achieve what they say they will? And, in my view, effective leaders are not afraid to take risks. In a sense they are courageous. People look to their leaders to manage the calculated risks. "That's why they are paid the big bucks." Business cowards do not earn respect, and hypocrites when discovered are mentally written off. Of course, not everyone wants to be in a tough decision-making position. True leaders do. Do you?

- It is hard for today's corporate jet-setting CEO to win the sympathy of the rank and file; it is far preferable to be recognized as someone who leads by example. That may mean making sure that people know she worked her way up the ranks and did her own bag carrying and photocopying, like them; it means eating in the company cafeteria sometimes; putting in the hours in the office; enduring an occasional lack of heat or too much air-conditioning. Effective leaders are real people. People want to be led—by a person, not a name. They want to trust their aspirations, souls, values, and feelings to a real person, someone they know is sincere and trustworthy.

  I have often found that people take pride in their CEOs' successes and even their perks. I know that every time I was on TV or was published in the press, staff members were proud to mention it to their friends and family in conversation, and they basked in our company's collective successes. But they also wanted to follow someone grounded in reality who walked their walk. In part, that's why a few civil words or conversation and perhaps an individual or group meal with any employee helps build effective leadership. "When I was speaking with the president," they will let drop in conversation, implying a host of things, starting with "we are on the same team and the president is a real person."

Leading by example extends, I believe, to demonstrating a healthy lifestyle. If the standard-setters in a company practice poor eating habits, I've said outspokenly in *Business Week*, "it sends a message to members up and down the organization that this is acceptable behavior. Staying slim is more than looking and feeling good. . . . The additional energy, sense of well-being, happier mood and attitude that one experiences when one is *bien dans sa peau* is good, efficient business."

- I believe women are better than men at the use of "we" rather than "I." Being humble is a characteristic of good leaders. They don't want or accept the credit for other people's work. At Clicquot, Inc., I was charged with overall results, not individual results or successes. Achieve the former and you can enjoy being lavish in praise and support of employees' work.

- Fundamentally, people want and will follow a boss who has integrity and honesty. Leaders are often tested and have many opportunities to confirm these essential character traits to the staff and set the tone for the company. They are people who keep their word. There's winning at all costs and then there's winning within the rules and winning honorably. Too many all-cost guys (historically they are almost all guys) have found themselves amid front-page scandals over the past decade, even in jail, and made Senators Sarbanes and Oxley famous.

- Though it is not an essential characteristic of an effective leader, a sense of humor is highly desirable. I frequently tell myself not to take anything too seriously, especially myself. It is a good thing to step back sometimes and laugh at some tense situations or yourself, or simply recognize the place and value of laughter in the workplace.

In the natural order of things, leadership skills are partly genetic. In the barnyard pecking order, there's always another ready to step up and fill a power void. That may be the case for chickens or sheep or, in the survival of the fittest, lions, but not in today's complex business world. Sure, there are some natural-born leaders—look to any sports team, professional or amateur—but there is also a great deal of experience and nurturing that goes into becoming a business leader today. Some skills and talents are transferable across industries and professions, but specialized experience is increasingly a requirement.

. . . .

MOI

In *Women of Wine: The Rise of Women in the Global Wine Industry,* a well-researched University of California Press book authored by Ann B. Matasar, I read about myself, my leadership and management style. "A tough, no-nonsense executive" caught my attention. Well, yes, true (though I was not prone to furrowing my brows and welcomed laughter). "No fan of job-hopping, she expects total loyalty from her employees and will not rehire someone who leaves. She promotes from within, using the motto 'the best grow, the rest go.' . . . Always optimistic and never scared . . . Mireille is persistent and finds ways to get where she has to go without letting gender become a hindrance. She wants her staff to respect, not necessarily love, her." Okay. Guilty on all counts. *C'est moi, bien sûr.*

The overall portrait is quite flattering, but what these somewhat out-of-context but true characterizations point to is the importance of knowing and accepting the leadership and management style of your boss. At the minimum, respecting it, if not loving it. Or find another boss.

I *was* a tough, no-nonsense boss, at least as much to myself as to our employees. How else could a woman excel in that environment and retain her self-respect? We paid our people well, nurtured them with lots of staff development and mentoring, and provided a great many perks. And I was certainly consistent and honest. People believed I knew what I was talking about and that I was not too proud to ask about things I did not know (especially of accountants, auditors, or attorneys, whose businesses, after all, depend on people asking them specialized questions). Our employees always knew where they stood and what was expected of them. I confess I did not and do not suffer fools gladly, and I abhor phonies who try to game the system. Laziness? Forget it. Over the years I heard my share of remarkably lame excuses. But I never turned to shouting, and, to quote from Ms. Matasar's book again, I believe "that people must avoid trying to do too much and must have equilibrium in their lives."

As a leader, a reality I learned about employees is that there are always some who think you are a lousy boss and some who think they could do your job even better. (They're basing their conclusions on what little they know about the job or without knowing the stream of confidential factors that influence a CEO's decisions for the good of the company.) The success of our company was unquestionable and consistently outstanding, and no doubt 80 percent of the employees respected and admired the vision, strategy, culture, leadership, and management of the company. I did not let the other 20 percent bother or divert me (and they were mostly a silent 20 percent, but surely they existed).

Here is another application of the famous 80/20 rule. That's the widely applied principle that divides the meaningful from the less important into 80 and 20 percent or, sometimes, 20 and 80 percent. Thus, 20 percent of something yields 80 percent of the results. You may have heard it expressed like this: 20 percent of our products account for 80 percent of our sales, or 20 percent of our stores or distributors account for 80 percent of our sales, or 20 percent of the staff is generating 80 percent of the output.

I have seen 20 percent of the staff creating 80 percent of the criticism or malcontent. You can worry about those 20 percent or focus on the 80 percent. Thick-skinned leaders can always listen to criticism and learn from it when appropriate, but also understand that there will seemingly always be 20 percent of just plain noise, so don't take it too personally or let it divert you from the more important foci. And, needless to say, eliminate the source(s) of the noise when you can.

The business lesson is: Grow a thick skin; expect and do not focus on the 20 percent of noise you will encounter. Don't invest psychic or physical energy on things you cannot control; focus on the positive.

My leadership style developed out of my personality, of course, and out of some classic characteristics of effective leadership that I either learned by doing or through reading about. But mostly, I learned or at least remembered what not to do by observing others—and they were almost exclusively men. As a woman I did not have many, perhaps any, role models. There was no one to show me how to assert myself without causing fallout. How feminine to act and still be effective? How to defuse stereotypical profiling and behaviors by male colleagues? How to speak softly and control meetings and get people to deliver on time and on target without having to resort to sanctions to show you are the boss? How to draw the boundaries of personal and professional behaviors in the workplace and business environs where relatively few women had trod? The list of complexities and subtleties is long, and the challenge for young women developing their own leadership style is a minefield without female guides and role models. Male bosses just don't get some of the challenges female executives feel and face. So, one thing I am sure about is that young leaders need their bosses to stand behind and support them and their decisions—the good ones and the not so good ones—as they evolve their style and effectiveness. Even the slightest perceived crack in that wall of support will be exploited by the doubters.

....

MANAGEMENT

I began this chapter with the observation that leaders and managers are not the same thing. This is not to say that managers don't do a little leading, but managers mostly manage people and outcomes. Management skills are not the same as leadership skills. Good leaders sometimes are notoriously bad managers. (I'll protect the names of the guilty.)

This is not a management textbook, and the essentials of how to become a good manager merit a fully developed, multifaceted treatment and not a magazine-style top ten list. What I want to share, though, are what for me proved to be three extremely useful principles or beliefs that served me well again and again. I am not counting the all-important point that I have already stated in a number of ways: Good people skills and communications skills are necessary for good management. You need to communicate effectively and be able to reach individuals in ways and at times that resonate within them.

The first useful principle: *Hiring is the most important thing a manager does* and is the sign of a good leader. It's about getting the right people in the boat, to use that common male metaphor. (I'm not of much use on a boat at all, I'm afraid.) On this ship of commerce, there is sometimes the debate of whether you get the right people on the boat, then set a course with vision and strategy, or start with the vision and strategy and then recruit the people. The latter makes more sense to me, but Jim Collins, author of *Good to Great*, finds that the former produces better results. For most it's an academic question, of course, based on the unlikely assumption that you are a start-up with no employees or you can take a going concern, fire everyone, and hire whomever you want. The reality in hiring is iterative, like weeding a garden.

The second key belief is tied closely to the first: *People are an organization's most important asset.* And the boat is moving, so *you constantly need a new mix of talents and skills* that people bring for the voyage. That's one of the important management lessons I learned: When you are an X-size company with X market share and X-type challenges, you need a crew suited for X. When you grow to Y, not everyone will be the right fit, and when you grow or transform to Z, the reality is that you probably need to take on a lot of new crew; it is not likely that all that many will grow from X to Z. For one thing, they will lack experience at meeting the challenges and managing a Z company. Start-ups, for example, if successful, generally outgrow the people and skill sets that got them launched. Back to the boat metaphor, if you are worried about the launch, the crew you need won't be picked for or have some of the skills to run the boat well on the high seas.

One of the hardest things to do as a manager is say good-bye to a good worker and colleague who has done everything expected to help you get your department, your division, and the company to where it is, but now does not have the right stuff to help you take it to a new level. Try explaining that, especially to a mid- or long-term employee. They'll probably think it is you and not them who is out of place. The reality is your company has outgrown them. It is not personal—you may like and respect them very much—but try telling them that convincingly on their way out the door. In the best of cases, the person can fill another role in the organization effectively.

A somewhat parallel situation is when there is an opening that a good employee thinks she is right for, but you think the company would be better served if it looked outside for more immediate skills and experience. Saying no to that person is similar to saying good-bye to a good worker, because when you pass up someone for a promotion, you are often telling them to get a new job or acknowledging that your decision means they will leave sooner rather than later. I had a charming and talented manager in communications and marketing who wanted the top job in that area before she was ready for it (I knew she wasn't ready . . . she didn't). She was also stuck with the classic situation of her peers and coworkers with whom she had "grown up" not seeing her as their leader. Sometimes circumstances just dictate that you need a fresh place and new start. Within a year she moved on, picked up enhanced experience, and with one more move had the job she sought. Time passed, and I am always happy when I run into her, and I think she is, too.

My advice for dealing with these situations and people is relatively simple (starting with a given, which is that you may never get them to appreciate your decision or perhaps ever again appreciate you). Don't rush to a decision—you may need to speak with them before reaching your final decision—but when you are confident in your decision, be firm. Don't give them false hopes that you might change your mind. Naturally, treat people with dignity and respect, and make it as easy as you can for them to land on their feet. Also treat them well in front of their colleagues, and do not talk badly about them after they are gone. There are personalities and personalities, so you need to customize your approach a bit (and remember that situations such as these will bring out elements in people you did not know they had). In the case of a long-term employee, you might have the heart-to-heart talk six months before s/he has to go, giving them time to seek a new position while they are still employed. But quietly keeping someone around who has one foot out the door is tricky and will not work with everyone. In a case when you know it would be better to have the person clear out their desk that afternoon, you may have to provide sufficient severance pay to ease their transition. And sometimes you have to tell people to clear out by 5 p.m., not because you fear what they will say or do to damage your department, business, and company, but because of what the impact of their presence over time will mean to their coworkers and the operations of the company. In the end, when dealing with people who are hitting their heads on a ceiling or who no longer fit the company well, the offer to serve as a good reference is always a palliative.

Let me return to in-the-boat talent and bring this down to the reality of on-the-ground hiring. First, the hiring you do is one of the most important tasks—perhaps the most important task—you will perform. Don't rush it. I have seen far too many managers rush to check off hiring on their to-do list. It is work and takes time and money and can be frustrating when you have an opening to fill and you and others are carrying an extra workload. Making the *right* hire is cost-effective, time-saving, and will make your life easier. So, if a candidate doesn't feel quite right to you . . . pass.

Second, realize you are not hiring for the long term, but the relative near term, say one to three years, and to fill a specific immediate need. Who knows if the position will even exist in three years or if the requisite skill set and experience will have evolved with the company? Pick the person who will be able to perform at close to full speed after no longer than six months. Hiring the best talent for the current situation is always the best strategy. And the best talent includes someone with a talent for getting along with you.

Next, remember that hiring is as much art as science. If you get it right nine out of ten times, that's a 90 percent success rate. Give yourself an A. Some of my hiring decisions turned out to be mistakes. *Ça va sans dire.* It took me a while in business to know that you should not expect the theoretical ideal of a 100 percent match; 90 percent still wins awards, whereas being a rigid perfectionist, ironically, focuses one on failure and can be self-defeating.

Finally, appreciate that after you have culled the résumés

down or HR has sent you some finalists, you'll be choosing among qualified candidates; that is, they will all have the skills and experience you require for someone in the position. A first interview can confirm that, but then the final interview is about picking someone, not learning if they are qualified. Input from a colleague who also interviewed the person may be helpful in getting a fuller picture, but in the end, if the person is going to report to you, pick the person you feel the most comfortable with.

I have a technique for discovering the real person. I hold the final interview over lunch or, occasionally, dinner. I usually ask the candidate to suggest a few restaurants (and their answers are revealing, as is everything that transpires). At a meal, you can see how awkward or polished they are, how relaxed and conversational they are, how knowledgeable they are over a range of topics, how humorous and genuine they are, and more. Mostly you can see whether you'd mind spending time and sharing business meals with this person, which is a likely proposition, and whether you can see this person representing you and your company in out-of-the-office business settings. It's eye-opening, and always beats reading a résumé. Sometimes meeting the spouse, especially if the couple would be relocating, is an important step as well. For most management positions you are getting something of a team, and you should know the support person, if there is one, who will be spending a percentage of their time talking and thinking about your business and, indeed, showing up at some business functions. For successful recruitment, it is important to ensure that the partner is comfortable with the move . . . and a little extra attention goes a long way. Plus, it is one more piece of input in your decision process.

. . . .

ORGANIZATIONAL TALENT

My third key belief in what distinguishes an effective manager is *good time-priority management.*

I used to devise metrics once a year to provide clarity and keep people focused on the outcomes expected of them in the best interests of the company. I had to do that, as a good number of our employees seemed to focus on what they liked or were good at, or otherwise appeared to work inefficiently, without direction. We had salespeople who would gleefully sell more of a particular wine than we had available to ship—and expect praise for it—yet seemingly forgot one of the key deliverables in our budget plan.

Those who through self-discipline spend the bulk of their time on what matters stand out. Effective time-priority management skills are not on the average college curriculum. Either you have acquired them through some form of spontaneous generation—perhaps figuring it out by the hard learn-by-doing route—or you need a good dose of staff development at your company, and a good manager who will mentor you along the way.

If time-priority management were not such an important but unrealized skill, Stephen Covey would not have sold millions of copies of his book *First Things First* and delivered countless presentations. It is a good, sound book, I'd recommend it, but I've learned over time that not everyone reads, or, at least, a lot of people need input from other media to absorb information. (I appreciate that's an ironic statement coming from a book author, but if you have read this passage, you belong to the class that does indeed absorb knowledge via the printed word.) If you want to reach a broad swath of your employees, schedule a mandatory workshop, or at annual review time make time-priority management a measurable outcome in key managers' personal development plans for the following year. I tried both. What I found worked best in terms of generating better awareness and application of time-priority management skills—just one company at one point in time, not a universal solution—was giving every employee an abridged audio version of Covey's book to listen to in the car, on the subway, or on a plane. Just getting people to see that they spend way too much time (and we are all guilty of it) on trivia, interruptions, and nonproductive activities and should spend more on preparation, prevention, planning, and relationship building can be transformative.

In a sense, time-priority management is a key to success and happiness. We don't have enough time in business and life, but achieving balance and happiness is due in part to prioritizing and using our time well rather than regretting how we spent our time when it is past. That's a management principle to live by.

8

ZEN AND THE ART OF BUSINESS(LIFE)

One day I was sitting in my Clicquot office in New York when a cold call came in from someone in London. The person wanted me to speak to a group of women about "my philosophy." I took the call. It came at a time when *French Women Don't Get Fat* was on all the British bestseller lists, and the caller turned out to represent a speakers bureau. Would I give a keynote address for a group of executive women at a conference outside London, a professional development retreat with an emphasis on time-life management strategies? Sounded interesting, so, after some more details and give-and-take, I said yes, with two conditions. One was that they had to serve our company's Champagne and the second was I would only do it if I could tag it onto the beginning or end of one of my monthly trips to Europe. It worked out.

The group turned out to be from a famous investment banking firm, and the young, bright women there were investment bankers near burnout. Indeed, the purpose of the posh retreat was for the firm to retain some of this high-priced, highly trained talent. Money was not the issue for these women. They were earning plenty but had no time to spend it. Some had country houses and cottages they rarely saw. Ditto kids and husbands. They did not want more corporate perks; even the luxurious retreat complete with spa services was stressful for some of them. They wanted their lives back. And apparently a goodly number were quitting to that end.

The need to find a balance between work life and personal life is not restricted to women, of course, and has become one of the great struggles among today's workers and working wounded, but it is especially resonant among women. The very expression *work-life balance* derives from conflicts recorded a generation ago by working mothers in their place of business. "Enlightened" companies such as the one sponsoring the conference and human resource departments increasingly are addressing the topic and exploring solutions because it has become both a recruitment and retention issue, a productivity issue in terms of health-care costs and lost time as well as bottom-line profit and growth return on investment, and it certainly can adversely affect customer service and relations. Moreover, it may well become an overall talent issue in America, as 77 million baby boomers retire versus 44 million replacements in the upcoming generation (though America has always relied on importing talent when needed).

Work-life balance has a lot more to do with you, though, than with your job or company. When the first labor laws for women and children were introduced in the United States, in 1874, the State of Massachusetts fixed an enforceable limit of sixty hours a week. (Many a week I would have welcomed that limit.)

Around the world today, the time people spend at work and at the office continues to creep back to yesteryear, when ten hours a day, six days a week were accepted in agriculture and industry. I don't believe all those hours today are always productive time, though. (When more women run the show, will there be as many 7 p.m. or 7 a.m. meetings as there are today? I doubt it.) What my executive colleagues in France were doing in the office at 8 p.m. was always a wonder to me. As was the fact that executives in Japan never left the office before their boss did. After a number of years I started consciously going home earlier (though not exactly early), in hopes of seeing my young staff wrap up sooner. There is always more work to do if you want to do it.

Hours in the office, away from home and a personal life, are one thing, but you must also add in the time and stress of the commute (I don't see how you cannot count that pleasure as part of the work cycle), which in New York can easily be an hour or more door-to-door *each* way, yet doesn't raise eyebrows. (I know a pair of attorneys who, after twenty years of commuting more than an hour to Manhattan, just bought a one-bedroom apartment near their offices and are astounded at how much of a positive impact it has had on their sleep . . . and lives.) With the Internet, smartphones, desktop video-conferencing, and other communication technologies, you are seemingly always connected with work, 24/7. Go to a hotel pool in the afternoon and listen to the business deals going on among people who are supposedly on vacation. That's also a function of the global economy, where international business does not respect local holidays, time zones, or people's personal lives. (At least twice a year I am awakened in the middle of the night by a phone call from someone somewhere who is hard at work and oblivious to the fact that I was asleep.)

Another contemporary factor that detracts from personal time and abets work time is that we lead such complicated personal lives. People with live-in relationships generally have to address the challenges of dual careers to a greater extent than ever before. I know coordinating schedules with my husband is a chess match, and when he's late or traveling, I too often fall into the mindless trap of more work. Net, net: Sixty hours a week over six days, as I hinted earlier, sounds realistic to me for an executive with significant responsibilities. Not only is it probably too much and unhealthy to sustain for years or decades, the real challenge for most of us in the present is how not to let it grow beyond such a limit, much less reduce it to a classic forty hours over five days. Even hourly workers are pressured to take overtime and exceed that limit—it is cheaper for a company to hire them than to add to the payroll—and then add in their commute time.

Couples have to make an effort at finding balance and the time to be together. Some solutions seem extreme, but they work. I remember sitting with a couple who both travel extensively for their jobs, trying to fix a date for a dinner together, which routinely means two or three months out. They pulled out their electronic calendars and started to call out dates and cities where each would be, then apologized and said, "You know, we have to schedule time together months ahead." No apology necessary; it sounded good to me, and Edward and I quickly sat down and blocked out a few days for ourselves. We also knew an extreme case, a brainy and intense woman who worked crazy hours in derivatives at a Wall Street firm. I am not sure why she couldn't predict her weekends, but she took to the strikingly costly and at times wasteful self-preservation strategy of booking the best suite at a top New England inn at least once and sometimes twice a month for about four months, knowing in advance that she and her husband would make it there perhaps half of the times, and the decision would be last-minute. What about the reservations? Sometimes she had to eat the bill for an unused room, a high price to pay for sure, but worth it and necessary for her to find balance and relaxation. When your relationship is one of your anchors and seemingly the most important thing in your life, you sometimes just have to pay—a form of insurance.

Edward and I had a rule that we would not be apart more than five consecutive days. We set that rule because one or two nights apart became six or seven as our international travel increased, and we found that simply unacceptable. Long separations did not occur all that often, but it meant that one of us would fly to the city where the other person was for a couple of nights, usually the weekend. I remember once coordinating plane flights from different cities to arrive within minutes of one another at adjoining gates in the Phoenix airport. The next forty-eight hours before we each took off again in different directions were more than worth it. I know perhaps it sounds like an unaffordable luxury, but looking back, I remember and value this wonderful romantic "mini-vacation."

Expensive, yes, and not possible for everyone, but remember, people who are on the road and in the air days and weeks each month build up a treasure chest of frequent flier miles. Happily, staying connected is easier today in the asynchronous digital world of email, voice messages, smartphones, and more. I simply cannot call up Edward and interrupt a business meeting (or, in lots of time zones, his sleep), and vice versa, but maintaining a sort of running blog for two, we are now more connected than ever when we are physically apart (it's a kind of flip side to the very electronics that can make us feel constantly at work). Not a substitute for seeing and feeling, but helpful in maintaining one's equilibrium.

If the exigencies of work keep you apart from your loved ones, consider it a prompt to make sure you schedule quality time when you are together. You need to spend time, not money: plan a long walk together, establish a go-to-a-movie night, take a fixed night out each month without the kids . . . bowling, anyone? *N'importe quoi.*

Corporations and the government have made good progress over the past few decades in embracing real-world work-balance practices, though largely of the family-friendly variety, growing out of the increase in working moms. There are better maternity leave practices (still not good enough), flex-time programs, employee assistance programs, on-site day care and child referral services, better sexual harassment policies and awareness, age discrimination laws, even some work-at-home options and sabbaticals. Still, stress in the workplace is not diminishing, nor is personal time on the increase. It seems to me these policies and practices have little impact on most employees. Look around— the demographic reality is that there simply are not that many coworkers with young children, and while it is great and essential to have built-in protections for them, there has generally been a sympathetic history and tolerance for the special needs of working mothers. That's not the main problem.

It is not possible to look to organizations for workplace policies to cover everyone's imbalances. We've seen a growth in counseling and training programs in work-life issues, and a steady increase in studies, books, and online resources. But they all point to the same obvious conclusion: One size does not fit all. Our situations are all (from slightly to vastly) different. Our needs and interests are different. Our hopes and responsibilities are different. You must create the optimal individualized work-life balance strategy for yourself.

....

ANCHORS

Every Saturday morning when I am in New York, I go to the Union Square Greenmarket. Here farmers and producers from the tristate area set up stalls to sell their organic and traditional foodstuff. Every "booth" has a portable white tentlike canopy to shade the people and produce from the direct sun and from the rain on rainy days, and sometimes even snow. Wind, though, can be the most prevalent element, and each of the legs of the canopy has to be tied down and anchored, often with heavily weighted bags at the feet of the legs, to prevent the protective covering with its armature from flying away and doing damage. All four legs need to be anchored. I've seen what can happen if even one or two are not properly secured.

These four support legs and the all-important anchors at their base remind me of what it takes to support a work-life balance. The four elements are: 1) good health, 2) a functional social network of friends and family, 3) a solid employment situation, and 4) time, space, principles, and policies for yourself. They work together, interacting in sometimes mysterious ways, and some stronger anchors can compensate for weaker ones, but the stress will become apparent then. Lose one of the anchors and you are left twisting in the wind and out of balance.

While inspecting and reinforcing your four anchors will result in a generally stable work-life balance, particularly stressful times and situations call for additional specific short-term strategies. Plus it is important to remember to maintain balance during rough periods, say, when periodic downturns in the economy can add stress at work and at home.

In the next chapter, I will offer some on-the-ground strategies for coping with work-life imbalances, but for now I'd like to stick to the higher concepts. It is always easy to get lost in the details, but it is the big picture that matters most.

....

STRESS AND HEALTH

The concept of having good health requires the least ink, but it is certainly the most ignored, until you get sick. Women in their twenties and thirties take good health for granted, and rightly so, as most are in the best health of their lives. Being stressed out is not being in good health, and it leads to impaired judgment, poor performance, and reduced immunity. Need I mention weight gain? Current research on Americans shows that nearly one out of two deals with stress by overeating or eating unhealthy food.

Stress can be productive, of course. It's nature's genetic defense against threats, releasing chemicals into our bloodstream that get our hearts beating faster, move more oxygen into our lungs and muscles, release sugars and energy from fat, and speed up blood clotting. One price we pay is that our immune system slows down. Our primitive selves cannot tell the difference between barbarians at the gate and a report due tomorrow. Some of us welcome the stress that drives us and energizes us to meet deadlines or complete special projects. But too often, like students at the end of an exam period, we get sick afterward. Our defenses are down.

While women's stress response works in a way similar to men's, it is even stronger with women, as they have higher levels of cortisol, a driver of a heightened state of chemical and physical readiness. In addition, changes in the female sex hormones estrogen and progesterone act like cortisol, so that prior to menstruation or at times of high stress, women become more vulnerable to everything, from the common cold to cancer to asthma.

....

Eliminating unnecessary stress is a good thing indeed. It even reduces belly fat, or at least prevents it, as recent studies have
shown that the stress hormone cortisol sends fat to the abdomen!
And big bellies are full of medical mischief.

....

CONFIDANTS

Whom do you trust? I am reminded of a passage in Matthew Ar-
nold's poem "Dover Beach" that my husband periodically re-
cites. "Ah, love, let us be true / To one another! for the world,
which seems / To lie before us like a land of dreams, / So various, so beautiful, so new, / Hath really neither joy, nor love, nor
light, / Nor certitude, nor peace, nor help for pain; / And we are
here as on a darkling plain / Swept with confused alarms of
struggle and flight, / Where ignorant armies clash by night."

To be *bien dans sa peau*, to achieve balance in life, you need
at least a small social network of people close to you whom you
love and can trust, and then a wider network of people you can
speak openly and comfortably with. I'm talking about the sphere
in which you can wear your most intimate persona, and no
matter what you may think, that is not the mask (persona) you
wear at the office or with coworkers. You (hopefully) wear your
own, genuine face at work, but it is still a different one.

Clearly a relative, partner, or spouse can fill the first role as
trusted confidant, though that level of intimacy can be achieved
with a close friend or two or a combination of these. We know
from experience and human psychology 101, and from endless

....

talk shows, that it helps to talk about the things that are stressing you, but you need the people at hand to do so, and that is when close confidants or a support network outside the office can do the most good. A collegial support group at work can be helpful with some work-related issues, but you need a circle divorced from work that from time to time can provide you with objective feedback and emotional support (not to mention play and laughter). Just knowing you have the support available is stress-reducing. For many, religious groups and leaders fill the role of or are part of a wide support network. If no anchor is in place, it is safe to say that your stress level may be higher than is healthy.

....

OFFICE FOOTING

For a lot of people, long hours in the office are a good thing. Work provides them—and all of us to varying degrees—with self-esteem, social interaction, and daily satisfaction, and fills other specific needs during various phases in life—whether one is single, married, divorced, has children or not, is an empty-nester or widowed. This is another reason why strategies for achieving personal and professional balance need to be individualized; they are not like a recipe with precise ingredients for your favorite dessert.

Your job and career is an anchor that is easy to test. Look in the mirror. Are you comfortable with what you see? Are you relatively happy with what you are doing each day at work? Can you see yourself doing the same sort of work for the next year or two? Is there a future that you want for yourself at this company? Are you proud of the company or organization where you work and what it produces? Do you respect your boss and senior management? Is the work challenging but achievable? Do you work collaboratively and effectively with your coworkers? Are you treated with respect and courtesy? Is the compensation competitive and fair? Are the benefit programs enlightened and supportive, especially HR development and support programs that are meaningful to you?

If your truth meter is mostly pointing in the yes direction, you probably have a job that's good for you at this time. If not, then you know what you need to do to improve your balance. One of your anchors is wobbly. Chances are you don't need this self-test to know that you have a decent job; it is a reminder, though, not to blame the job for all your stress and imbalance. It is an invitation to revisit your priorities, time management, and other anchors.

....

YOUR PERSONAL ZEN

While all four of the anchors that I believe provide the necessary life-work balance are equally important, the "you" anchor is the one that can most easily get lost in time-priority management strife. You have to go to work, you have to talk to your mother or partner, you have to feed yourself and your family if you have one, and eventually you have to go to sleep. But so often you don't think you have to do the things that are for yourself, maybe taking a walk, reading a book, getting a massage. That's a mistake, one it took me years to recognize. We probably all know it empirically, or hear or read about it, but caught up in life and business's exigencies, it came to me slowly: I had to experience the rewards and reinforcements of the little things I came to do for myself that made me feel good in the moment and better about myself overall. Once realized, this combination of *amour propre* (self-esteem) and *amour de soi* (self-love) becomes who you are.

Many of us try to be good to everyone else and devote all of our time to that. It's part of the superwoman ethos. Nurturing others before ourselves appears to be built into our genes. Too often we feel guilty if we do for ourselves ahead of others. Too often we define ourselves and our happiness through others—our spouse, our children, our parents, our boss. Making time for yourself and not feeling guilty about putting yourself at times ahead of others may seem oft-told advice, but do you hear it . . . and follow it? If you do the best you can at the time, ban the self-abuse—you've earned the right to no regrets. A more appropriate self-query is: What makes *you* happy? What makes *your* center hold? So what if your husband or boyfriend likes to mountain-climb or fly-fish? Good for him. You don't have to. Your sister likes to Rollerblade, good for her. What's good for you? I have a friend who began competitive ballroom dancing at age fifty . . . without her husband.

You have to make time each day to let go of judgmental thinking and live in the moment, let's call it a Zen moment. Lose your self-consciousness, clear your mind, and accept the present.

You can feel the stress melt away. It's your time. In almost any activity you enjoy, you can lose yourself and find yourself. At the minimum, schedule some regular "beach time," *plage de temps* in French, a space of time to retreat to on a daily or regular periodic basis, so that you can achieve a healthy balance of pleasure in life. It can be found listening to music, or even doing mindless chores. It can be found turning off your smartphone and Internet for a regularly fixed period. You can let your mind fill up with anxieties and vexing stress or, with a bit of practice, you can learn to head to the beach. Sometimes I read fiction or listen to Italian lessons on my iPod or do yoga exercises and meditation or listen to or play music. Music literally soothes you by synchronizing your body's rhythms—heart rate, blood pressure, brain waves, and breathing and bringing them to healthy levels. Find your special hobbies, pursuits, moments. They're healthy.

THE NOT-ALWAYS-SO-GENTLE
ART OF COPING

During the past decade I have begun most mornings with a walk before breakfast. It is one of my most valued "strategies" for controlling my day and mind. It simultaneously wakes me up gently with a bit of exercise and serves as a Zen moment to clear my head. Afterward, I simply feel better and more positive about approaching the rest of the day. When the weather is horrendous, I substitute twenty minutes of yoga, something I used to do more of before adding the ritual walk. I did neither in my twenties and thirties (though I've always been a walker). You have to find what helps you achieve balance as the episodes and stages in your personal and professional lives demand.

When did aggravation lose currency and become stress, and

when did stress in the workplace and at home become epidemic? Coincidentally or not, it has transpired as women have gone to work and climbed the educational and corporate ladder within our recent generation. Within the past couple of decades, four out of ten people have said they often feel stressed, and overall, eight out of ten workers in America feel stress on the job. No surprise.

Everyone has stress, some of it is helpful and good for you, some of it mildly addictive (why do people ride roller coasters?), but worrying about stress is, well, stressful. Dealing with stress can be stressful as well, especially because you cannot eliminate it all. So, my basic approach to it is to follow the classic advice of identifying and treating the underlying causes . . . but in phases. I am a believer in change *peu à peu* ("little by little") since drastic changes, including lots of changes made all at once, are often the sorts of modifications that don't stick.

Find and address three stress producers, then another three, then another three, and then, no matter what, declare victory so you stop creating more stress for yourself through the cure. What's success in reducing stress? Would you accept a 15 percent reduction? Thirty? Fifty? Get real, 50 percent is major surgery, such as changing careers and environment (which creates stresses that take months or even years to subside, yet may well be worthwhile in the long run). I believe five to ten "adjustments," depending on their order of magnitude, generally are enough for you to claim victory. Call it your short-term plan. (It's another example of the 80/20 rule.) A sustained short-term plan for coping with the stresses in your life can take a year, have various phases, and require an annual compass check before hitting the restart button. When you are especially stressed out, a short-term plan should be an immediate plan, of course—as in the next five minutes, by the end of the day, by next week.

What causes stress for you? As you are aware at least from this book, I am a big believer in "knowing thyself," which requires some objective, personal inventory. I believe, for instance, that by learning what your personal eating offenders are and reducing or eliminating them, you can easily shed five or ten pounds. Perhaps you don't realize that you eat a bowl of ice cream several nights a week before going to bed. Or that the yogurt you snack on each day is loaded with corn syrup, calories, and artificial flavors. I always liked the line in *Casablanca*, "Round up the usual suspects." It is a good place to start when conducting a personal inventory and works to reducing one's waist or one's stress . . . or both.

What I suggest is that over a couple of weeks you jot down the triggers of your stress and anxieties, those things that flood your arteries with chemicals and get your heart beating rapidly, the things that cause you to behave in ways you don't like. Don't make this a mental list. Formalize it. Take notes. I am confident that everyone can reduce their stress with less effort than they imagine—we let the stupidest things stress us. Also, remember that time-priority management is one of the best stress-busters. Of course, if you need to lose eighty pounds, or are severely depressed, or are stressed beyond the point of being able to function at times, professional help should be a necessary part of your solution. That said, here are some specific coping strategies beyond those I've already shared.

....

BON VOYAGE

What's on my stress list? Travel is right up there for me. For someone who loves to travel and has to travel extensively for business, you would think that's an odd item to cite. Not if you've been at an airport recently (as in, anytime in the last twenty or thirty years). I love to have traveled, but not necessarily to travel. That is, I like it once I get to my destination.

Has an airline ever lost your luggage? If so, you probably dread checking bags. I don't, because I only use carry-on luggage. How is it possible? Easy, especially after the airlines lost my luggage twice in one summer many years ago, once on the way to a wedding. Never again. I have flown millions of miles around the world since then with a wheeled carry-on suitcase and a large handbag that fits on top of the luggage, which in turn fits into an overhead bin. So, it is doable. You have to pack smart and make some clothes do double duty. I have an Issey Miyake pants suit that's a wrinkle-proof featherweight I always add to my suitcase, along with a few scarves that can turn a black or another solid-color dress into a number of outfits.

Not checking bags saves me a lot of time and stress checking in, and it's wonderful to be able to arrive and pass out of the airport without delay. No more watching the luggage conveyer go round and round and worrying if my bags have made it.

But I have another trick. There are times when I need a gown or more shoes and bags than can fit in my carry-on. Sometimes there are books and files that weigh me down. I FedEx them to my destination. Do it sufficiently in advance and you can have a confirmation they have arrived before you even leave. That's peace of mind and a ticket to traveling light. You may be thinking it's expensive, though. Not really, considering the price of a plane ticket and a hotel room and, nowadays, sometimes a fee for checking a second or even a first bag! So the cost is relative, and what I ship is not heavy but bulky. For their return trip, I can send them at a slower, lower rate, sometimes even regular mail. And you know all those meeting reports and packages you get at conferences you don't want to throw away but never really want to see again? I mail them, too. I feel almost light-headed walking out of the hotel or meeting.

Last summer we invited a string of guests to visit us in Provence, and four couples arrived without their luggage. Eight missing suitcases! Great unkempt vacation for them, courtesy of the airlines, and a booster shot for my resolution never to check luggage.

Did you ever panic over not being able to find your ticket or passport or perhaps your jewelry? Join the club, but who needs that stress? The simple trick is to always pack and replace these items in precisely the same place so you always know where they are—perhaps a little cloth or leather envelope for travel documents kept in the same pocket of your suitcase or pocketbook: perhaps a colorful drawstring bag for your travel jewelry stored in the corner of your suitcase. Pills and prescription drugs? Perhaps in a cosmetics bag, but in today's world of inexplicable plastic bag security, keep some for peace of mind in your pocketbook and the rest in your suitcase in a container you can easily put your hand on. You get the drill: order, routine, and discipline. If you are a hopeless packer, I recommend reading *Colin Cowie Chic;* he is wonderfully fanatical (and sound) on travel preparation and compartmentalization.

I am the sort of person who always likes to be on time or early. Blame my mother. So, getting to airports on time was and is always a little stressful, considering the traffic in most major cities. As I got older, I decided I just didn't need the added stress, and what was the point of the extra twenty minutes at home? Now I leave with plenty of time to spare, and I don't always know what I'll find at the other end. Delays are the bane of the business traveler. Get delayed and rerouted enough and you develop a defense mechanism. I travel with a book, an iPod, a cache of fruit and nuts as emergency food, perhaps even a boiled egg if I'm expecting a long flight, and figure I am being given the gift of found time to relax. I try to enjoy myself. I'll get to my destination when I get there . . . mind over matter. What's the worst thing that can happen? The flight is canceled? You miss a meeting through no fault of your own?

Another strategy I eventually adopted was to stop flying the red-eye to wherever. For years I did it and was exhausted for days afterward when I returned, yet did not miss a moment of work. On the contrary, I seem to have squeezed two workdays into one. Then I started to notice all of my male colleagues flying business or first class during the day, not during the middle of the night, even flying ahead by a day or two "to adjust to the time zone changes." What an idiot I had been. That's a good example of when I could have used a bit of mentoring . . . someone to coach me on how to slow down, not speed up.

As a businesswoman traveling alone, there are safety precautions that one must make to reduce risk and anxiety. More than once I was stalked, including once by a taxi driver who had heard me on a radio program and waited outside to pick me up. Scary. Use common sense. But don't get neurotic—I don't—just fix an eye on prevention. On the usual security checklist: Stay at a good hotel, don't give out your address to strangers, don't go out after dark alone, order room service, secure your room. Know where the emergency exits are. Check in with someone periodically. Carry a phone and remember to pack the battery charger. You don't need more stress.

....

OUT OF THE CLOSET

Clothes can complicate one's life, no question. Packing proves that. Do you start your workday stressed by what to wear? A lot of women when they're late to work blame it on not being able to decide in the morning what to wear. You probably wear the same five or ten outfits anyway, why do you go through the same mental gymnastics each day looking at and contemplating clothes? And if you have a hard time getting out of the house in the morning, you don't need this dilemma. Here are two simple stress-busters. Before going to bed, decide mentally or physically what you are going to wear to work tomorrow. Simple, and it works. And next, swear off the 110 percent rule for closet capacity. You have heard the advice that if you have not worn something in a year, get rid of it. It is sound advice. Practice it.

....

Something you might wear once in three years isn't worth saving. And a little room in one's closet is mentally liberating, to the point of perhaps feeling good about adding a new outfit each season or twice a year.

....

DORMEZ BIEN—SLEEP WELL

I saw a huge sign across the windows of a store on the Boulevard St-Germain in Paris proclaiming, *79% des Français se réveillent fatigués . . . et vous?* (79% of French people wake up tired . . . do you?). It got my attention, and made me think, yes, perhaps on New Year's Day . . . and if that many people in France wake up tired, then 109 percent of the people in New York City must. It turned out the store was part of a chain that sells health and wellness products, and the sign was a come-on for a light that would wake you up naturally and agreeably (*naturellement et agréablement*). Thus you would not be brutally awakened by noise (as in an alarm clock?) and so seemingly you would be less tired??? I did not buy the light, but I bought the general point about sleep.

Health is not like the weather—you can indeed do something about it. In terms of achieving balance and reducing stress, nothing is more important than a good night's sleep. Again, you've heard that, but do you practice it? It is well established that most people need seven or eight hours of sleep nightly, and while some thrive on six hours, almost everyone I meet in business seems to think they are special cases and can get by on four, five, or six hours. Who are they kidding? At night they are just on information overload and cannot stop doing whatever to get to bed regularly at an appropriate hour. You know these people; many walk around carrying superjumbo containers of Starbucks coffee to prime their pumps all morning. Their work often suffers, which continues the cycle of stress. It may mean longer hours to get things done or more hours and stress to make up for mistakes.

If you are waking up in the middle of the night thinking of work and can't go back to sleep, consider it an alert. Writing middle-of-the-night Post-its? That's a close encounter of the unhealthiest kind.

Sleep is the most neglected state of being in American life. We think we can cut corners, push ourselves to the limit, but we're only fooling ourselves. Lack of sleep makes us listless, decreases our sensory alertness, and increases our stress-response hormones—which only makes it harder to fall asleep at night and creates a vicious cycle that's tough to break. A good night's sleep is vital to our lives, both in and out of the office.

The test for sleep deprivation is a simple one. Lie down when it is not bedtime, close your eyes, and relax. If you fall asleep within a few minutes—surprise, you need more sleep. Sleep is nature's way of wiping away the stress that builds up over the course of a day and prepares one to face the new dawn somewhat energized and rejuvenated. The rules for a good night's sleep are basic. You were probably taught them in elementary school. Sleep in a dark, quiet, cool room with a crack of fresh air. Follow one or two rituals that help you wind down and prepare you for sleep—perhaps a systematic cleansing of your face or drinking a warm cup of herb tea. Go to bed at approximately the same time each night. *Et voilà.* Then it's safe to drive your kids to school each morning.

....

MANGEZ BIEN—EAT WELL

Starting the day on an empty stomach is almost as bad as starting it tired. I have written extensively elsewhere on the value of three "meals" a day, however small the portions may be, so I won't belabor the point here, but I want to reinforce just a few ideas, starting with the fact that we are what we eat. We cannot perform to the best of our ability at the office if we do not eat well. Eat healthy, be healthy . . . and happy.

I do not buy it when people say they don't need breakfast. I can't help it, I think they are poor time managers who haven't factored in a few minutes to take in a little protein and carbohydrate—say a slice of bread and a piece of cheese, washed down with a little coffee or tea. Want the ultimate quick, minimalist breakfast? Three almonds, two bite-size portions of cheese, such as Jarlsberg, and the juice equivalent of a single orange, no more—or better still, eat a single orange or another piece of fruit. Plus, of course, a glass of water. Surely you can spare a few moments. And I cannot help thinking those breakfast abstainers are the people who are walking down the street or driving a car while sipping coffee and wolfing down some sugary pastry. If they were thinking that skipping breakfast would help them keep their weight down, they can forget it. These are also the people who often need a "snack" at eleven a.m. or who binge at dinner. Having no breakfast almost always invites poor food and eating habits, and a sugar-covered doughnut washed down with coffee only invites a severe sugar crash and a poor attention span. Ditto for lunch, when even a few nuts and/or dried fruits will save one from bingeing later, and also aid us in staying focused and productive. Plus, a few moments away from the work at hand will restore one's mind and balance.

Dinner, though, requires commitment. Again, if you don't fuel your body during the day, you'll tend to overeat (and perhaps overdrink) at dinner. Then what? You fall asleep in front of the TV (and TV watching in the first place correlates with weight gain) and destroy your sleep pattern—among several other undesirable outcomes you often regret later. Sitting down and eating a balanced meal in the evening is a surefire way to support a balanced lifestyle. If you dine with a loved one(s), it is important social time. If you are alone, you should remember to eat at a table, dine slowly, and put your knife and fork down between bites. Remember the maximum pleasure is always in the first three bites, concentrate on the pleasure of the food. Avoid multitasking—no reading, TV, or loud music. A little soft music can complement a good meal's benefits, enhancing enjoyment of the present and cleansing the mind.

Remember, too, we generally eat too much for our sedentary lives. So, gradually reduce your portion size, especially as you get older. The supersized portions we have come to expect are late twentieth-century phenomena. Practice the 50 percent solution here as well. Serve yourself half of what you think you want and need, and then if you really want and need more food, feed yourself only 50 percent more of what you want, and then reassess. I was a great one for having eyes bigger than my stomach whenever I passed a pastry shop.

Travel is no excuse to abandon good eating habits; it is actually a call to arms to remember and enforce your good practices. And by all means, avoid eating airplane food just because they've put it down in front of you. The last thing you need is two dinners, one on an airplane. Ask yourself if airplane food gives you pleasure . . . or tastes good? Drink an herbal tea or glass of water, or a few glasses, depending on the length of the flight. Water will keep you hydrated and feeling less hungry.

One last word for now on food and health. Believe it or not, I do not believe that everyone should be skinny. I have said again and again that everyone should feel comfortable in their skin, and if that includes a few extra curves à la Renoir, so be it. In fact, that's probably healthy. However, there's no denying we live in a world of increasing obesity, and for many overweight people the unnecessary weight causes an enormous range of health problems, unhappiness, and stress—from epidemic type II diabetes to high blood pressure and coronary disease. So, depending on your size, it must be said that losing five or ten or twenty pounds could have big, big medical and psychological benefits. You owe it to yourself. Stress raises one's blood pressure. Sound nutrition and healthy body weight reduce it.

....

TAKE A BREATH

Here's the quickest short-term strategy I know to address a sudden onslaught of stress at the workplace or at home: breathing. This is a simple relaxation exercise. Close your eyes and breathe in deeply from your diaphragm for a count of, say, five, and out for a count of ten. Focus on your breathing and ban other thoughts (or at least acknowledge them and put them aside). Repeat a half dozen times. Visualize the tension in your body—in your head, neck, back—dissipating. At your desk you can do it a couple of times a day or as often as necessary. Amazing.

When you find yourself at a moment of needing a deep breath, it is also a good time for a mini reality check. I ask myself what it is that is making me feel so stressed, and is it worth it? Then, as I have done many times, I apply my mantra, asking, "What's the worst thing that can happen?" More often than not your answers to yourself release a good deal of air out of the tense balloon, like a therapeutic exhalation.

Conscious breathing is the easiest and most basic form of meditation; it can help us refocus in a moment of stress, enhance our energy levels, and even help relieve minor aches and pains, such as tension headaches.

In your overall strategic plan for managing balance in your life and reenergizing yourself, find a technique that can regularly assist you: yoga, meditation, jogging, tai chi, perhaps even volunteer work. Those are things our grandmothers did not teach us, but they lived in a different world.

Some of these techniques involve movement, and there is no

question that incorporating movement into your daily routine is highly beneficial. Some call it exercise. Farmers never worried about it, but if a daily visit to a gym works for you, it is still exercise. For me it takes the form of incorporating movement into my daily activities. I take the stairs rather than an elevator whenever I can, which is several times a day. I walk up escalators and walk a lot, including my Zen walk in the morning. I do yoga. I like the feeling and benefits some semi-rigorous exercise provides, and look forward to bicycling and swimming. I am not obsessed, however. I try to live a healthy lifestyle.

....

"*MOI*" TIME

In the last chapter I mentioned the importance of scheduling some daily "beach time," as a mind and body palliative. I want to reemphasize the importance of "you time" in achieving a healthy work-life balance, but let's also call it "my time . . . *moi* time," because that's what it needs to be for you. One of the horrible imbalances I see all around me, and indeed have seen in me, is the rut of weekdays for work and weekends for a personal life. In France we have an expression, *métro, boulot, dodo,* meaning subway, work, sleep. We've all been there, done that. Operated on autopilot for days at a time. If you wait till the weekend to break the routine and to "have a life," you set yourself up for some disappointments. There's not enough time. Weekends pass too quickly. You're exhausted and don't get to what you want to. You have such high hopes and expectations; the reality becomes

....

sobering or even depressing. Or you binge on whatever—eating, drinking, shopping, family excursions, talking—then it is back to *métro, boulot, dodo.* My advice is, not only do you need to schedule beach time during the week—the operative word is *schedule*—you need to schedule "you time" during the weekend as well and stick to the schedule. Once again, it is a time-priority management and balance issue, not just a time issue. We have a fair amount of control over how we spend our time.

I know an executive couple with two children who made a rule always to sit down and eat a formal, unhurried dinner together on Friday evenings. It involved sacrifice and discipline, lost business sessions, and tedious travel arrangements, and the kids simply had to accept that until they graduated from high school, they were not going to talk with or go out with friends on Friday evenings, at least until the leisurely family dinner had ended. They made it work. It was a core component of the husband and wife's "social network of friends and family" anchor, and I know for the husband it was also his special "you" anchor.

....

THE WONDER OF ELECTRONICS

We live in a glorious age of a global digital economy, with new time-saving, pleasure-producing electronic aids at our fingertips. Or do we? Don't all those electronic gadgets—smartphones, laptop and desktop computers, iPods, digital audio and visual recorders, combinations thereof, coffeemakers and alarm clocks—

add a hitherto new stress storm to our lives along with efficiencies and pleasures?

Something in the corporate world where I dwelled that we come to take both as a necessity and for granted is the help desk and IT. When I moved over to my writer stage, computer infant that I am, all too often I found myself lost, stalled, and, yes, stressed. Well, my solution eventually was to hire a help desk and technician. Seems I wasn't alone. Small offices and work-at-homes all have outsourcing solutions for their computer needs. Sometimes it is a relative or friend. Mine is a company with a high-tech name and a smart guy I'll call Giles. In reality, it is one guy partnering with a few like-minded lone rangers who share an office and occasionally back one another up. Giles is professional, conscientious, courteous, high-priced, and good. He is also stressed out.

One beautiful, sunny December day, thirty-year-old Giles arrived at 9 a.m. sharp and looked a mess. I assumed he had spent the previous night at a club imbibing too many firewater concoctions and stayed up late. Such are the New York stereotypes we project. I offered him coffee. How about some breakfast? He declined, saying he couldn't eat, as he had not slept at all. I did not get that logic, but to my "wow" he answered he was burnt out. At his age? He explained he had probably made the wrong decision working on his own. He knew he didn't like being in an office and even less reporting to a boss, and with his unusual computer skills he knew he could go on his own and earn a good living. A year or so later, he feels he not only has more business than he can deal with but, more important, many highly stressed and demanding customers ("bosses") who cannot perform their business without his magic . . . as they remind him, with constant calls and text messages, whenever they have a problem. And problems are the name of the game. Meanwhile, his new wife sees what's coming and so has more or less given him an ultimatum: Let's talk, spend more time together, or else . . . Not something he's quite figured out how to deal with, at least not without trashing his overscheduled business. Talk about stress. His one concession and stress-buster thus far is completely shutting down connectivity for twenty-four hours each weekend. It's a start.

Seeing his stress, and the stress involved with connecting with people at dial-up and online help desks to solve some of my minor technology problems, was, ironically, comforting to me. Not just because I had displaced some of my stress to him, but because it was a reminder of the relatively unavoidable stress we can expect will be associated with the installation and operating "challenges" (not problems, right?), including crashes and malfunctions, of all that electronic equipment we "must" have. It is the stuff of panic attacks for some. I also share the Giles story in part as a contemplative mirror to our own lives and as a sign of our digital times when our work-life balances are under attack by the "connective" electronic devices that can make us crazy. I mean, tuning in a movie or recording one on cable or satellite TV can be absurdly stressful, at least for me. I don't need that. (All those buttons and remote controllers . . . *quelle horreur.*) We need to prepare our defenses and coping strategies for the stressful situations electronics create.

I've learned to live some moments without email. (As we all used to!) Systems go down but my world does not. Once upon a time there was only snail mail for business, then eventually faxes, or the phone. Speaking of the phone and the stress of constant connectivity and using modern technology, I proactively retreat for calming periods, shutting down my cell phone for long stretches each week. That's a time-management luxury and coping strategy in my current stage of life. I also try to check my email only twice daily when I can. Sometimes it's not an option, and certainly not everyone can do this in an age when so much business relies on email and its variations, but maybe signing out of email for just an hour per day, or not checking your email on weekends (you are entitled to a day off) would relieve some stress for you. What are your ways of dealing with the wonders of electronics?

....

VACATIONS

As someone raised in Europe, one of the hardest things for me to come to understand was the American attitude toward vacations. Two weeks a year? You've got to be kidding, is the reaction of most Europeans. Unless you are self-employed, six weeks for *les vacances* is considered an inalienable right for a French person. There's a deep-seated belief among the French that vacation is part of the natural balance and is necessary in order to recharge one's batteries, and that self-indulgent "play" is a psychological necessity to well-being. I agree. Perhaps it is in my DNA. A lot of people make fun of the hedonistic French and their endless vacations—I often tell people the French are so fixated on their personal time that the plan for their next vacation is a commonly overheard conversation, even when they are currently on vacation. However, France is not a European outlier. German workers, for instance (and no one has ever called German workers or the German economy slackers), average thirty paid vacation days, compared with an average of ten for American workers.

I have met a lot of Americans who do not take all of their vacation days. It is a curious badge of honor for some. What are they thinking or denying? Is work such a big and essential anchor to their lives that they are afraid to be away from it? Are they afraid people will discover the company can live without them? That's a given. Virtually no one is irreplaceable. That sobering fact is reinforced daily on business and front pages with CEOs of brand-name companies coming and going, sometimes voluntarily, often not, and many a company does just fine in relatively short order. It doesn't take much work experience to see that employees go and business continues to get done. You may think you are special, and you are in your own mind. Are you worried about other people depending on your being there to get their work done? Plan ahead; many companies with liberal vacation policies set aside certain mandatory vacation periods, say, a week at year's end or two weeks in the summer, so that business shuts down to a skeleton crew and reopens with full staff. That's good time management and planning.

If you are concerned about achieving a healthy work-life balance, then rejoice in your vacations. They are one of the few structural fixes we have. Take your full time and don't feel guilty about it. I always preached to my staff to take personal time and vacation time. It makes you a better worker and person. I was surprised that as a leader I had to set that tone.

....

LAUGHTER

When I first came to live in New York, I was amused by two little phone applications. (Today we have the Internet.) One is you could order food—mostly pizza and Chinese—for home delivery almost any hour of the day or night. Pizza or egg rolls at midnight. Wow. I did not order either, but that I could was both comforting and amazing. The other was that you could dial a joke. There was a special number with a different comedian and different jokes every day. What a world. I did use that number now and again. Who doesn't like laughter, perhaps the greatest stress-buster?

On the short list of things within your control to combat stress and achieve greater balance, adding a regular dose of laughter and entertainment is a no-brainer. And today we live in a just-in-time, on-demand world. Make that work for you.

It's easier to create and experience humor outside the office, and that's why I believe "play time" is important to a company's culture, whether scheduled as a company party or event or even during a national sales meeting. Sometimes, though, it pays to think "out of the box" and with malice aforethought inject some laughter into the sober execution of workday business. It's a bit dangerous, of course. Not everyone finds the same things funny or has their heads in the same game you do, and when a joke falls flat, if you are the teller, your hard-earned reputation is exposed and perhaps vulnerable. Still . . . no risk, no gain.

In my early days as a CEO, one of my nightmare projects of the year was to present the annual budget plan in Paris. No matter how much advance preparation, exchange of documents, and iterative actions, there was always a showdown. I always wanted approval to spend more, often on communications and marketing or approval to earn more revenue by being granted a larger share of available product at the expense of other markets. This was the moment for my best and last argument—my audience was a room of (French) gentlemen who seemed numb for the occasion, knowing well the budget would be tight and there wouldn't be much in terms of concessions. It seemed the economy was never going to be better next year. From their conservative economic viewpoint we were seemingly always in recession or there was always the threat of a recession that would dampen results. I exaggerate only slightly.

Perhaps it was a sign of the times or of French culture, but when it came to the moment of truth, people did not look at slides or charts, they looked at me and listened to my oral argument (remember about communication skills being the most important business skill?). Of course I had a few colorful slides to wake people up at important moments and visualize the compelling picture at year's end, but my presentation was almost all talk. One time, before pulling out a graphic from my bag of props, I gently slowed down by taking extra time to set things up, made a long pause, took a deep breath, and rolled up the sleeves of my classic woman's business suit in the most natural way, only to reveal tattoos on my lower arms—most notably Veuve Clicquot's iconic anchor in black and orange, symbol of the company and its proud history under Madame Clicquot. I continued amid a little buzz of male reaction, then our chairman started laughing and another member of the board said, "*Mais vous êtes complètement folle*" (You are nuts). (What they did not know is that these were washable tattoos, left over from a recent "Yelloween" party in New York. They figured I was committed to the extreme.) I smiled and continued as if nothing had happened but noticed I had everybody's attention and the previous tension and detachment in the room had evaporated. I presented a comparatively short plan, and at the end they all clapped and my chairman said, "*On y va*"—Let's go. . . . The budget was accepted without a problem and they all laughed when my chairman announced the official "OK" with "*Vous êtes une sacrée bonne femme*" (You are a heck of a woman). I could have taken that as a sexist remark, but I gladly accepted it as the high compliment he meant it to be, about as strong as I ever received. It being Paris and a French business meeting, people's minds turned immediately—if they had not done so earlier—to (a bubbly) lunch, where I finally told them that I wasn't that crazy, as the tattoos would wear off within a few days! They liked that part even better. I had to send them all fake tattoos.

(BUSINESS)WOMEN AND MEN
ARE DIFFERENT

Are you troubled, as I am, by the propagation of the myth that women have to be monsters to succeed and sit in the corner office? That is not about women helping women, and I see people jumping to conclusions about top women based on such stereotypes. Whether it is cause or effect or both, many of these stereotypes are played out in the movies. How are women portrayed as corporate executives in memorable movies of the past decades? Amanda Priestly (played by Meryl Streep), the self-absorbed, she-witch diva in *The Devil Wears Prada*. The untrustworthy, sly, and manipulative football team owner Christina Pagniacci (played by Cameron Diaz) in *Any Given Sunday*. How about Meredith Johnson, the tough, sexy, harassing computer company boss (played by Demi Moore) in *Disclosure*? Or the self-centered, people-using-and-abusing boss Katharine (played by Sigourney Weaver), whom Tess overturns in *Working Girl*? Or, earlier in the prototype, the cold-blooded, obsessed producer (played by Faye Dunaway) in *Network*? I could go on. All abusive, egomaniacal, driven, and pretty much one and the same. Is this today's new stock character in our contemporary version of the *commedia dell'arte*? And all played by top actresses. Are these the best roles and role models? Don't nice, talented women finish first, not last? Where are the fair, smart, savvy, and nurturing types?

For sure, people's behavior can be startling. When you think you've seen it all, you are just beginning, and it often isn't pretty. The workplace is full of surprises. The work of any manager in business is managing people in the process of achieving business ends, but people often have their own ideas and personality when it comes to being managed. Dealing with authority figures brings out the worst in some. They fight direction. Others want to be left alone after getting their marching orders. Still others need constant reinforcement and return and return again for approval of action after action. Some of their behaviors you simply could never imagine ahead of time, but you can classify them and identify them in some way that "enlightens" and prepares you for what you must face. When it comes to women versus men, here are a few of my personal takes.

TEARY-EYED

Women are said to be more emotional than men. Mostly true, I think, especially if you discount anger, but how can you? Hot tempers in the office are somehow forgiven in men (who are perceived as "in control" or "demanding") but not women (who are perceived as "emotional").

Tears are enjoying a revival, it seems. It is okay to cry at work, some believe. Not me. Remember the movie *A League of One's Own*, about an all-women's baseball league during World War II? The manager, a drunkard and former Major League star played by Tom Hanks, screams at a weepy player, "There's no crying in baseball . . . there's no crying in baseball." Well, I say there is no crying in business. Not over lost opportunities, poor performance, freak accidents, lost baggage, hurt feelings, whatever. Sure, it is accepted and even respected when a man or woman cries over a significant personal loss or accident or perhaps gets teary-eyed over a retirement. That's warm, sincere, and human. Life does have a way of taking precedence.

But at a business meeting? Tears and associated behaviors are often seen as a sign of weakness, a sign a person can't keep ideas and emotions separate and is perhaps vulnerable or unstable. It's an "I gotcha" moment in any subtle negotiation or power struggle. I never wanted to be in that position. I steeled myself against it. (I cannot tell you precisely how not to cry at work, but I advise you to figure it out for yourself before the time comes when you want and need to control your emotions at a business encounter. Till then, if necessary, excuse yourself and head to the bathroom.) Crying certainly can be an awkward, embarrassing moment that sends people away to calm themselves and regroup before continuing. It is not a good career move to be the instigator of such moments either. Perhaps worst of all, a lot of people see tears in a woman as manipulative.

In the business-as-war metaphor, a male conceit I don't accept, business leaders don't want to go to battle alongside someone prone to tears. Who does? There are plenty of other compatriots to choose from. And this is, sadly, a women's issue . . . men get cut some slack on tears and even a few favorable nods for occasionally tearing up.

....

A WOMAN LEARNING
A PRESUMABLY MAN'S WORLD

When we started Clicquot, Inc., in 1984, the wine world I entered in America was a tough, essentially all-male environment in America. (And in France it was truly an all-male club.) I worked in part with old-line distributors, as I noted earlier, and with many liquor salesmen who sold wine as a sideline, at a time when America was just waking up to wine at the table. I did not have an on-the-street sales background and didn't know how the business really got done. But I learned quickly. How was I going to work with those hard-nosed distributors and tough ex–liquor salesmen? I wasn't going to entertain them and their best customers at strip clubs, as our top manager in Germany did on his junkets to New York. I had to find my own way of developing a relationship with them. In some cases I'd take them to a steak-house and afterward to a jazz club. And I could be a tough, tough negotiator. How would that go? No problem. I always controlled my decibel level, even when delivering the "riot act." I was always treated respectfully and professionally, always found win-win situations and alternative entertainments. And, surprise, surprise, those sales guys always wanted to meet me. I must have been a curiosity.

Like many men who cut back on profanity in front of women, these guys rarely swore in my presence (in the car some-times, when they did not have to look me in the eye and could not hold back). They also were a bit more reluctant in business meetings to say no to my face. Indeed, I learned that a yes in person was sometimes just an avoidance of controversy. Men might say yes to a woman at a meeting rather than engage in a heated (and profane) disagreement as they might with a man. Meeting over, they went about doing business their usual way. I learned to follow up my significant business meetings with a written understanding of what was agreed upon, and then held everyone accountable for living up to the agreements. Having things in writing almost always helps.

· · · · · · · · · · · · · · · ·

COMMUNICATION STYLES

Men do not ask for travel directions, right? That is a universally accepted truth. Men seem to see asking questions as a sign of weakness or failure. Women ask questions. If you've ever served as copilot, you've done the asking for directions. Of course, there are exceptions and special cases and few absolutes, but there are some gender-specific communication styles that are well researched and documented. Being sensitive to them in the workplace can help avoid some serious miscommunications and help you in achieving your and your company's goals and needs.

In any argument, negotiation, or discussion, it is imperative that you know your audience. Here are a few classic communication gaps and styles I've learned to recognize and address in keeping workplace dialogue productive (not that I was always successful).

As I've noted, women like to ask questions and gather a lot of information before tackling a task head-on; men like to plunge in, letting the ends justify the means. In my experience, men typically do not read instructions. (Forgive the overly simplistic generalization for discussion purposes.) Ever watch a man load some software, hook up some home electronic unit, assemble something that came in parts? They generally will read the instruction only if they have been unsuccessful at first intuiting the correct path. Each gender often doesn't understand or perhaps appreciate the other's approach, which leads to frustrations and miscommunications that can carry over, counterproductively, into other elements of a working relationship, including emotional outbursts or confusing subcurrents.

We have known since the days of Aristotle that communications have both logical and emotional charges. Men are great at delivering a sound message while obliviously hurting another's feelings. No one likes to have their feelings battered, but women are more vulnerable to—let's call it heightened emotional sensitivity. Be sensitive to your audience and, when possible, use analytics—data-driven decisions or strategic points—to defuse a discussion and get back to the business points. And perhaps be a bit understanding; normally people are not out to abuse you emotionally; usually they are just poor at communication. What else is new in gender relations?

In doing business internationally, the need to minimize the emotional content and threat of unintentional slights in a discussion that should maintain or build a strong personal working relationship is magnified. A lot of global business is built on understanding and respecting another culture's values and protocols. For example, in the Middle East, the word "yes" in a business discussion means "maybe." In China or Japan, "yes" might very well mean, "I don't want to hurt your feelings or offend you, so I am saying yes but don't mean it." Also in the Middle and Far East, there is a range of almost ritualistic practices, from the exchange of gifts to seating arrangements to the language of greetings and toasts, that needs to be followed to make for a comfortable relationship. Only the naïve and impatient jump to the chase, oblivious to unintended insults and damage to business. In those cases, we hope our partners are savvy and forgiving, just as we need to be to act in our own enlightened self-interest when crossing some gender communication gaps. Realizing that attitudes toward women, in particular, are not the same in some parts of the world as in America or Europe should figure in your relationship building, including the realization that it is in one's business interest not to attempt single-handedly to change a culture.

Women are more comfortable with and prone to talking about their feelings than men, but being overly talkative in business settings can become awkward and shut down conversation. Be alert to that. We have to control ourselves more in the office than at home.

Another fundamental difference in gender communications that is close to my heart, and one I expect will become increasingly apparent in the workplace, is that women like stories. They are in no hurry to finish telling a story or listening to one; men are. I cannot tell you the times I've lived through with men trying to end a conversation in mid-story so as to get down to business. That leads to impatience on the part of the sender and the receiver, not a good thing. I suspect that men's tendency to want to get to the point and want it now is why business books written by men seem so dry to me, and why, as a woman, I write the kind of books I do. Engaging and illustrative stories are good business tools.

Men speak louder than women, interrupt more, and generally speak out more in business meetings as well as use more declarative statements. Both to be noticed and to be taken seriously, women do need to contribute at staff meetings and seminars. But make every word count. Here again, less is more. We are not impressed by the outgoing person who has an opinion on everything and lets everyone know it. The person with a clear and incisive comment wins respect. And as for appearing competent, confident, and convincing, I always found that softly repeating my point in a variety of ways in one-on-one or group meetings worked. Again, what I tell you three times is true.

Oh, and men swear a lot more in the workplace, and it can be effective in team building and morale boosting if used in a competitive sports style; however, profanity is another double standard. Men swear and are tolerated and even respected; women who swear like men are often seen as overly asserting themselves, vulgar, verbally aggressive, or followers (imitators), not leaders, and are not respected by men.

....

GOSSIP

Women and men have different takes on gossip of the tabloid kind and of the office variety. Gossip is much more a women's thing, and in this digital landscape, with its easy, anonymous access, gossip is becoming dark, dangerous, and sometimes akin to the palace intrigues of Louis XIV. People's lives can be brutalized by snarky rumors and unflattering fantasies spread widely by others. Author Erica Jong believes "gossip is the opiate of the oppressed." The slightest moment of celebrity opens one up to all sorts of attacks, including comments on various parts of the body and mind. I'm amazed. It appears that it makes little difference if the author knows the subject or person they are writing about, or, if they do, that they are taking great liberties with the truth. I certainly wonder about the motives and rewards for a person who zips off nasty comments in blogs with great eagerness. In accepting her 2009 Golden Globe award, actress-comedian Tina Fey said, "If you ever start to feel too good about yourself, they have this thing called the Internet. You can find a lot of people who don't like you." *Oui.*

In the workplace, gossip and the grapevine can have negative effects. As I was a woman working in a mostly man's business world and served on executive committees with almost all men, or attended mostly all-male corporate retreats and corporate training sessions, I observed that men simply do not revel or indulge all that much in speaking about people behind their backs. Criticisms are out front, and "gossip" is exchanged with laughter in mind, not cruelty. However, when the inevitable "who is sleeping with whom" comes up, the woman is never referred to favorably.

In the office, rumors and groundless criticism waste time. As a leader you should rarely address rumors or anonymous attacks (rightly called cowardly); it just rewards the initiators and draws attention to you and the rumors, which people then may believe have some credence. If you have a mentor or a trustworthy supervisor, that may be a good time for her to step in if your name needs clearing, and put an end to the unprofessional mischief. Plus, it could save you or another good worker from hurt feelings and from having to leave the company due to an unhealthy environment. If you are at the lower end of the corporate totem pole, simply do not contribute to a negative culture by engaging in or accepting such poor, counterproductive business behaviors. Behind-the-scenes targeted attacks meant to diminish a person are workplace gossip, unacceptable and really a form of violence. Most companies' email policies and personnel practices rightly come down hard on abusers.

....

SEX AND ROMANCE

The "casting couch" or sleeping one's way up the ladder is, thankfully, dying in myth, rumor, and reality, in part due to sexual harassment policies and enforcement as well as fear of exposure, via digital media and within corporate ranks. So, too, are groping and verbal obscenities. If you are old enough to read this, you have learned to some degree by now how to repel unwanted sexual advances. I lost my first job out of college in Paris because I refused to "French-kiss" my boss. I was naïve to accept an invitation to discuss business and my performance with him at a local café and then a ride home. I should not have put myself in that position. Later a former colleague told me he wasn't dangerous, but it was a routine operation with him, *comme l'armée* (like in the army), and there were always new recruits. It was a good job, but no regrets.

Sex in the workplace will always be with us, and it is dangerous for business and people. Some women are willing to trade sexual favors for opportunity and some men actively send out invitations, but is this another male thing? Women are much less likely to covet and reward sexual favors.

Romance in the workplace, however, happens. Surprise? Not really, if you are spending forty or fifty hours a week at the office or at evening meetings and traveling for work. You are meeting people, married or not, and generally they're "safe" people who as coworkers or business associates have been somewhat screened and already have a number of things in common with you.

....

Office "affairs" have a lot of potential for damage, especially to women. They surely distract the lovers from company business, can form power blocs in the firm's decision-making processes, and can produce nasty and abusive breakups, which sometimes force coworkers to take sides and thus destabilize the work environment for lots of people. Like it or not, when an office romance turns public and bad, it is the woman's reputation and potential for climbing the corporate ladder that is damaged most. Gender discrimination relating to office affairs persists.

Of course, office romances sometimes end happily, in marriage. I have had couples meet and wed where I've worked and live seemingly contentedly thereafter, usually with one spouse leaving the company. If your office romance is getting serious, it is probably wise to clue in your supervisor, who will eventually find out anyway and won't like being surprised and one of the last to know. S/he might even help steer you through difficult waters, including reporting conflicts, and manage the office gossip that could cause irrevocable career problems.

When it comes to office affairs and romances, here are a few commonsense yellow lights: If you want to avoid entanglements, don't envision yourself with a coworker, which can start you down a dangerous slope. Think thrice before trading an hour of intimacy for the risk of losing the stability and relationship(s) you have built up over years. Don't kid yourself, if you play the seductress or flirt childishly, you are advertising your availability and/or playing with fire. Don't put yourself in dangerous or tempting situations, and certainly don't lower your defenses inadvertently through alcohol, drugs, fatigue, or what have you.

As someone working in the Champagne business, I had to rescue and later counsel young and sometimes not so young staffers of both sexes who had had too much of a good thing and were about to risk making fools of themselves and perhaps damaging their careers (as well as potentially offending our clients and hurting our business). I have always reminded myself that I was working, not playing or partying.

....

MONEY

Americans point to money and work as the leading causes of stress. Gender differences relating to money and work are part of that picture.

Men definitely keep score with money. Salary is key unless you are a billionaire, when your net worth and comparative national or world ranking are how you keep score. (I am amused by how mega-rich men—recession or no recession—cannot help mentioning their private jets, including the models, which are meaningless to me. Bigger is better is the standard.)

For women, salary inequity is the issue. With all the advances in the marketplace for women in the past generation, the gender gap in salaries has not disappeared. Men in America working full time overall earn about 25 percent more than women (one survey I saw put the figure at 77 percent, and those numbers are always a year or two behind the present). The "overall" is somewhat understandable in that men are more willing than women are to travel or relocate for better pay. Men are also more likely to take positions with greater financial risk but potential for greater financial return, or even to take on hazardous risks for bigger bucks. Also, men if sufficiently educated are more likely to select higher-paying careers than women. Put another way, women are more likely to sacrifice money for other benefits, such as time, balance, fulfillment, and security.

This nagging inequity means that based on the U.S. Department of Labor statistics, women's salaries as a percentage of those earned by men in the same profession have not moved close to parity. Indeed, in sales they are off by about a third, in medicine by about a quarter, and even in technology they are off by about an eighth.

The simplest explanation for this is that women, unlike men, do not like to haggle over money and do not negotiate effectively when they are hired or during salary reviews, and the salary differential tends to be compounded over time. No question that women fear negotiations more than men. One survey reported that women are two and a half times more reluctant to challenge their salary when they have the opportunity to negotiate for more.

Learning to negotiate is one of those skills you may need to develop, but along the same lines as a man? Adopting stereotypical male behaviors cannot be the ideal for a balanced workplace. Moreover, women who negotiate and appear assertive like men are perceived as less nice than a woman who is more "feminine" and does not haggle, and not someone a man wants to work with. So, such behaviors can be self-penalizing. Gender bias has not been erased.

I always went into my own salary reviews with a carefully reasoned benchmark range for what I thought I was worth to the company. Whatever position you hold, it is not too difficult in these online days to get a benchmark range for what comparable positions pay, though be sure you adjust for location and benefits and are realistic. Lots of professional organizations publish compensation surveys. My reviews usually worked out fine, but I occasionally had to resort to my iron-fist-in-a-velvet-glove approach when I thought I was not being treated financially as a male would be. Pointing that out often won the day, but be careful how you raise the point. I usually did it as a rhetorical question. "If we were advertising for this position and a male was the finalist, what would you be thinking of compensating him?" I always hired and compensated people sex-blind—based only on experience, talent, education, and market rates. So there were no gender pay gaps among our employees.

Therein may rest the inevitable solution for moving women's salaries to parity with men's. As more women move to the highest management levels, including the corner offices, the gap will simply disappear, perhaps in part because women are much more comfortable with and likely to negotiate with another woman than with a man.

Another gender-specific pay problem has emerged, however. As more and more women are moving into the well-paid professions once dominated by men, they are generating more income than their husband or partner. Not all guys respond well to this. Remember, men often measure their success and build their self-esteem around the adequacy of their performance, keeping score by dollars. Even if it is their loved one who is succeeding, they seemingly cannot overcome self-doubts, fears of perception and respect, insecurities; and thus a heap of stress is added to an all-important relationship.

Other than being sensitive to this and talking things out and being patient with one's mate, I don't have an easy solution. Certainly do not apologize for what you earn or feel bad about it. You should be proud. Hopefully, there will be other reasons for your partner to feel good about himself and over time to accept this financial balance.

A lot of it has to do, of course, with his being comfortable in his skin and job and overcoming caring about what other people may think about him when the two of you are introduced or seen together.

I am a firm believer that women who work should have reasonable control over their income. They don't need permission to make most purchases, and one's companion should not scrutinize small- and medium-size purchases, whether clothes, gifts, household items, or haircuts. I've always had my own checkbook. It just worked out that way, and over the years my direct-deposit paychecks went into that account. I had a checking account before I was married, and kept the interest-bearing account and the credit card that came with it after I became married, though I turned it into a joint account, just in case. My husband kept his account and cards. For years we'd reconcile after a month or two of bill paying. Savings and investments were joint. During many of those years, I earned more than he did—and I am happy this was never a problem for us—so I simply paid a larger percentage of some core monthly expenses. No big deal. If your or your spouse's purchases become a problem for the other person, I know some people address this by setting up free-spending limits of, say, $250 or $500 per purchase before consultation with their partner is required and thereby avoid unpleasant month-end discoveries. Still, I recommend keeping your personal cookie jar reasonably full and your expectations within means, because it feels liberating and reduces stress.

As in so many areas, we create much of our stress by wanting too much and setting unrealistic objectives. Financially that translates into wanting more than we can afford, which can introduce strain and decisions and sacrifices that one partner or both resent. You know, dinner and a movie versus saving for a new TV. A vacation now versus saving to purchase a home, or a bigger home. Big and little, his or hers, there can be problems. All I'll say about that is live within your means, and remember that material goods don't buy long-term happiness.

....

MENTORING

I began this book invoking the glass half-empty personal belief, through observation, that the poverty of business mentoring for women is a shame. That's partly a result of seeing some women from whom you'd expect more being poor or indifferent mentors to other women. Overall, though, I have not seen a whole lot of mentoring, period. People seem just too caught up in themselves and in meeting the personal and professional demands on their time to pause enough to embrace others for others' sakes. And, while I may not have the exact percentages to back it up—but plenty of individual experience—men are often better mentors to women than women. Shocking? And survey after survey shows that women prefer to work for men rather than women. Why? Sure, a female colleague will teach you how to use the latest piece of software or will sit with you when you are down. Is that mentoring? I wonder at times if it isn't a form of quiet gloating. Women will come together over pay equity issues or some workplace issues, but that isn't mentoring either. Senior women will give a talk to other women when they are asked. But devote systematic attention to the personal and professional growth of a colleague over an extended period? Rare, in my experience, and even rarer for those who have made it high up the ladder to look back down. Too busy? Perhaps. Jaded by their experience on the way up? Perhaps.

Don't get me wrong. Just because I am scratching my head and trying to figure out what's the story with mentoring, I do not want to propagate negative stereotypes or go from a little specific part of gender roles in business to a sweeping generality about women. I remain a champion of women in business. I am convinced that in most cases they are better workers than men and bring huge talents to the office that will transform how business is done in the coming decades. Time after time I hired and gave women a chance in a man's world . . . to good results. We bring feminine values to the workplace that need to be recognized by men—and also women—as assets rather than liabilities.

Troubled, however, by my own observations about mentoring, I tested my hypothesis again and again with businesswomen in different fields and types of companies. They reinforced my belief. "When I joined the law firm," one successful attorney confided in me, "there were only three women who had made partner. And they never spoke to me. A couple of men took an interest in me, though they dropped it once I had moved to the middle ranks and was generating noticeable business."

Certainly there are men who want to demonstrate how fair and open-minded they are and who go out of their way to help and even champion women and minorities. But I rather think men more than women are comfortable with competition and not threatened by it. Perhaps it is because they grow up playing ball in the schoolyard and get used to winning and losing and moving on. If they or their team lose today, they accept it, and if they aren't as good a player as Johnnie, they accept that and, if anything, want more than ever to be Johnnie's friend after school. Women often see other women as a direct threat to their getting what they want.

I am not sure how I'd prove that scientifically, but it is a nasty form of jealousy, for sure. There was a recent survey of working women in France who were asked, "What is the percentage of women who would not hesitate to betray a colleague to get a promotion?" The response was, 30 percent would betray a colleague. If you have achieved any degree of personal or business success, you know about jealousy, as it's far more likely to negatively affect women than men at the office. (I don't believe in it as a genetic trait but one that's nurtured.) When men succeeded at their jobs or got justly promoted, it was always clear to me why it happened to them and not someone else. Cream rises to the top. When a woman got promoted, I always sensed a chorus of "why her and not me?" I know some of the women I associated with in business resented my success and perhaps thought they could do my job. Perhaps in another world, but through a confluence of time, talent, and opportunity, it was my job. No one said life is fair.

If women are going to rise to the top, we need to build trusted communities of other high-achieving professional women and learn to ask for help from one another. There is some truth to the old adage "it's lonely at the top." For women, it can be even lonelier often, if you are one of the few women in a roomful of men. Apart from mentoring or networking, oftentimes successful women need to ask other women in similar positions questions perhaps only another woman would understand. Say you're the only woman at a high-powered gathering, even some sort of board meeting, and you've found that some issues are not being addressed or questions answered from the perspective you bring. You think the rest are not quite getting the true picture. How best to handle this? Perhaps you would like to fill a senior position in your company with another woman; you can turn to your trusted community for help in sourcing the position. Building these trusted communities can help women better learn to help each other and dispel some of the jealousy (and stereotypes) that has populated the past paths of successful women.

EATING FOR BUSINESS AND PLEASURE

I confess to sometimes thinking and talking about my next meal while I am eating the present one. It must be a French gene. I know a lot of compatriots who do it, too. And while it gives me pleasure, it also takes some pleasure away from eating in the present. So, I learned to control myself, especially as it can annoy my husband or other dining companion who is trying to focus and enjoy what's on his or her plate. On the other hand, business meals are often about building relationships and finding common interests and grounds for discussion. And if someone brings up a meal past, present, or future, I'm happy to engage.

You may be surprised that I've included the topic of eating for business and pleasure—and included recipes!—in a business book. Why? Because men haven't included the topic in business books before? Men certainly exercise their expense accounts in restaurants for business, and many entertain customers and colleagues at home. It is part of business life. "Eating for business" is common at every level of corporate life. And just because eating comes naturally, do you think you don't have anything to learn about the soft skills that go into it as part of business and professional growth? They are real skills that should be developed, and some people have exceptional knowledge in this area that distinguish and advance them. Let's see if there are any important lessons to be learned that will make you a more effective businessperson.

Besides, you have to eat. It can be one of life's greatest pleasures—it is certainly one of mine—and should be a key component to a healthful balance in business and life. After all, you can't avoid it, it soaks up so much of your time, and breaking bread is such a time-honored business and diplomatic practice. Why not be good at it? Whether dining out or eating in, there are a range of seasoned practices that can simplify your life, minimize your stress, and maximize your pleasures. They begin, though, with the acceptance that eating well is worth it.

For me, eating well is part of my brand. It's me. Food, of course, is one of those endless mysteries where the more you know the more you realize you don't know. And through cable TV, the Internet, and globalization we are assaulted by mind-boggling names and flavors. Just twenty-five years ago in Paris, the restaurants were almost exclusively French, with the key distinction being French regional cuisines. You might find a Vietnamese eatery in a section of the city, but, say, Italian? You could count the Italian restaurants on one hand. Not anymore.

As it has turned out, I am not intimidated at all by restaurants; *au contraire*, outside of home, they are some of the places where I feel most comfortable (I recognize that might make me seem odd to some), but it is understandable considering a lifetime of daily professional dining. Restaurants are a great place for a businesswoman to hold court, and I can help you circumscribe a comfort zone there. Thereafter, I want to share some thoughts on personal eating habits, and then provide some recipes and tips on home entertaining for business and pleasure.

But first, I want to assert the following truism: Entertaining is an act of friendship and cooking is an act of love. And here's a classic case where self-love is not only acceptable but desirable.

....

BUSINESS ENTERTAINING IN RESTAURANTS

Recently I invited two women I had not previously met for lunch at a relatively grand restaurant in New York City. Both highly accomplished professionals raising families in the suburbs, they had not eaten at the restaurant before and, indeed, did not frequent restaurants like this one often. I did not know that beforehand, and I was certainly not attempting to gain any advantage by choosing the playing field. It was not that kind of lunch. I simply love the food and modestly sized portions there. One guest arrived just before me and one just after me, and a question that broke the ice was, "Should I go to the bar or to the table

....

when I am the first to arrive?" It was a reminder that there are only good questions and that if some people fret about something seemingly this inconsequential, defuse it before it rolls up with a host of other little things into real anxiety.

Simply put, if you are the hostess you should try to be there first and go directly to the table. Use the free time to glance at the menu and wine list so you have an idea of what you might order and can free up your mind for your guests. If you are the guest and arrive before the host, the answer is not so simple. If you arrive roughly at the appointed time, then go to the table. And if pressed by the waiter to take a drink, order water or pass. Ask for the menu. If for whatever reason you as host or guest are going to be late, call the restaurant and leave a message at the front desk or send a text message (though following good business etiquette—and sometimes restaurant edict—means turning off your cell phone at the table). Reaching out can make all the difference.

Nowadays in America, there's the mild awkwardness of the handshake versus air kissing in greeting. People always kiss when they meet in Europe, on the street, in the home, or in a restaurant. Men or women, no matter. When I came to America, almost no one kissed in public, and especially not strangers (or nearly so) in restaurants. That's changed in the cities, it seems, at least in more upscale settings (a sign of globalization?). People look to the person in charge or the leading woman to take the lead. My preference in America is the handshake at a business meal or with a person I am meeting for the first time in the office.

If it is a kissing moment, you'll know—someone will take your hand as in a handshake and pull you toward them—and then it is right cheek, left cheek, kiss the air, and a don't-touch-and-spread-makeup moment. Sometimes, usually in America, it is only the right cheek. These social customs are like dancing. Then get on with things.

People look to the host to seat them, which is relatively straightforward. Generally if the dinner is somewhat formal and the number of guests more than four, the "most important" person sits on the right of the host. Then something like boy-girl-boy-girl follows, with the host paying some attention to seating people together who will stimulate conversation. In the case of a banquette, tradition has women sitting on the banquette and thus usually facing into the room. Men get to face the faces of the women . . . and the wall.

For business dinners, a lot of people do not have the luxury of commuting home and back after work, so they stay late at the office and arrive early at the restaurant. Then a seat at the bar, perhaps with another guest in the same situation, is a preferred path. If you run up a bar bill, pay it yourself before going to the table (unless you are drinking water), but don't run up a bar bill before a business dinner. Instead, a glass of wine at dinner will help you relax. A classic story recounted by the great gastronome and *New Yorker* writer of a generation ago, A. J. Liebling, tells of a visit to a celebrated French restaurant in Connecticut, where he discovered the wealthy clientele sloshed before sitting down to dinner. Liebling reports that it had been years since the diners had tasted what they were eating, and the disillusioned chef-owner from France had "taken to bourbon-on-the-rocks." The food was not very good, and the *spécialité de la maison* "was jellied oysters dyed red, white, and blue," about which the *patron* commented, "at least they are aware of that . . . the colors attract their attention."

My mother was a wonderful home entertainer, and seats at her lavish Sunday lunches were highly coveted. She had a rule, though, before such meals: no hard liquor. "It numbs your palate and your mind," she used to say. Business meals are not Friday nights out with friends.

If you are the host, you ultimately pick the restaurant and should try to accommodate your choice to your guest(s) and the purpose, of course; however, I always consider letting the guest participate in the decision by throwing out a couple of suggestions, signaling the type and price I have in mind, but then asking if there's someplace she'd like to go. Or asking, "Do you have a couple of suggestions?" It's a win if you can take business guests to a place they've "always" been meaning to go. By all means sound them out on some of their eating preferences or practices—I have made the mistake of taking a vegetarian to a steakhouse! This isn't how it always goes— some business associates I know well eat anything and like to go to the newest food destination on the scene, provided it is not too noisy for conversation, business or otherwise. So I honor them by scoring a reservation at some new, hot, or sublime eatery (or all three in one).

Here are two related rules I have for business entertaining

in restaurants. The first is, unless you are especially comfortable with your guest(s), do not go to a restaurant where you have not eaten before (advance disclosure of exceptions helps) or, if you are in their town or city, to a restaurant that they cannot vouch for. You can be very unpleasantly surprised by poor or inappropriate food and ambiance, and if you picked the restaurant, it reflects upon you. You don't want that, and you don't want your business guests to feel anything but pampered and special. The second rule is to become a regular at two or three restaurants, probably varying in style and cuisine, where you can count on some personal and perhaps special treatment. For an important business meeting, including when you want to make a good first impression, these are safe places to dine. How do you become a VIP at a good restaurant? Simple. Eat there periodically throughout the year and tip generously. You can jump-start such a relationship by eating two or three times in a month at a restaurant. The staff will quickly learn your face and name. And, of course, you'll be treated much better and more warmly than a stranger who walks through the door. It's good business.

As the hostess paying the bill, you have some responsibility to signal what's appropriate to order and put your guests at ease. On one end of the spectrum I've said, "Order anything you want" (knowing in the extreme there's caviar or truffles to be had at enormous premiums) and thereby signaling *carte blanche,* or "Would you like the tasting menu?" signaling it's okay to have a big meal with multiple courses. Most often, I say, "I'm going to have X as an appetizer and am thinking about Y as a main course," or just "I'm going to have an appetizer and main course," thereby telling my guests that two food courses, not one or three, are appropriate . . . and I leave a decision on dessert for later. Since a lot of people watch their diets, and I am saddened to hear "I'll have a salad to start with the dressing on the side" at a top restaurant (is that eating for pleasure?), I sometimes say "I'm going to have two appetizers, one as a starter and one for the main course," signaling not to worry about the norm, as I am going to practice portion control and if you wish you can, too. Indeed, I usually go the small-portion route.

When guests ask me to recommend a specific dish since I've eaten at the restaurant before, I try to avoid that responsibility, unless the restaurant is celebrated for a particular dish or two, and say so. One way to deflect the question and still be of help is to ask the waiter, "How's the Z tonight?" That initiates your guests into a decision-making conversation.

Once the menu is decided, then comes the wine selection, which can be a worry for a lot of people. *Bien sûr,* the right wine in moderation lubricates minds and tongues in a good way and can elevate the food experience. (Note, as the host you must not imbibe beyond your reasonable limit. This is business.) And the choice of wine can be flattering to your guests. Don't worry, here are four common situations and tested approaches.

Well, three approaches, given the fact if you know your wines and what you are doing you don't need any advice. Case closed. Order the wine and move on, setting everyone at ease. But rarely would you know the intricacies and delights of a restaurant wine list as well as the sommelier or waiter. So, if you are feeling at least a tad insecure, say to the waiter who took your order, "We're thinking of a red wine [or white and red wine if it is a grand meal or lots of people and different food choices], perhaps the [fill in the blank with any red wine you know or don't know in your price range]." The result will go something like this: "I'll send the sommelier over," or s/he is knowledgeable about the wines at this restaurant, so the waiter will suggest one or two others in your price range. S/he doesn't know your taste, but trust the waiter. They will know what other people have enjoyed, will know some good values on the lists, and will not steer you wrong. It is not in their interest to do so. Plus, it takes the pressure of a good choice away from you. The sommelier will follow the same path.

The second situation involves a wine geek at your table. He or she will have strong opinions about what to drink. Treat him or her as the sommelier. "I'm thinking about this red," and unless s/he is dull or arrogant, your guest will pick up on the price category and find a wine in it that will please them. Order it. What if they insist on something beyond the price range you are thinking or your budget or expense account will afford? Order it if at all possible. You are the host, and the customer (or guest) is always right. Over time it will even out . . . and you don't have to invite this wine geek to dinner again.

The third case is when you are the guest or you invite your guest to choose the wine "cold turkey." It takes the pressure off you and is gracious, but the person in the decision-making position is on the spot. I learned years ago a savvy strategy from a wine writer who was invited out all the time and asked by suppliers to pick the wine. Order the second or third most inexpensive wine on the list. If the restaurant is wine-friendly, it will be good. You will appear modest. And if the waiter, sommelier, or host thinks the wine is a mistake, you'll hear it via a gentle suggestion of another choice. Then let the host or guest choose, whichever you are not. You've fulfilled your obligation. The host may well feel inflated by upgrading your choice.

So, you've enjoyed the business meal, how do you handle the check? If you are the host, you should pay, period. No tossing credit cards into the bill tray or last-minute negotiations. As a guest, I've negotiated in advance to pay for the wine bill, when I wanted to be sure we drank our Champagne or one of our wines or perhaps to mark the evening with a special bottle. Normally, you (your company) are paying the bill. Unless you've worked something out in advance among colleagues, the rule of thumb is that the highest-ranking person from the host company picks up the tab. The something that sometimes gets worked out in advance is when the CFO or a PR-marketing person puts the dinner on their account. What I often worked out for myself is to get up late in the meal and settle the bill, then return to the table. Not signing a credit card slip in front of guests is a nice move.

ENTERTAINING AT HOME

Entertaining for business at home—the business ritual of break-ing bread with a customer or client, a contact, or a boss in your home for a meal or just "cocktails"—can be a special, winning move. And fun. It is a shortcut to building a personal relation-ship, is remembered and appreciated, and flatters the guests. You don't need the finest china or even a fully appointed dining room, you just need a will to please. And what's the worst thing that can happen?

Despite entertaining in restaurants my entire career, I also made it a practice throughout my life to entertain at home. When I did, it often made a powerful impression on many guests, who remind me years later of what we ate or said. Many of those oc-casions are strong memories for me, too, stronger certainly than many a business meal in a restaurant.

In *French Women for All Seasons* I wrote extensively on en-tertaining, but what I did not say—*j'ai oublié de vous dire*—is that it takes only three routines, three dinner menus with collat-eral effects, and a little practice to entertain at home successfully for your entire career. One or two tries and you have it down for life, and then you can play variations on the same theme. It is that simple. Nothing to fear.

The venerable gastronomic writer Brillat-Savarin said, "To invite a person to your house is to take charge of his happiness as long as he is beneath your roof." True, and before I share some thoughts on food and menus, here are some preliminaries on set-ting the stage.

When you entertain business associates, it is of course not the same thing as entertaining close friends or relatives, but the responsibilities for the host are similar. Here are some tips:

- Be yourself. Smile. Show that you are having fun and be gracious and generous, making your guests feel welcomed.

- Don't try to overdo it or you'll be set for failure. Simplicity is best both with your theme/décor and food.

- Planning is key. Lists help. Avoid catering, and personalize by trying to make at least two-thirds of the meal yourself in order to cultivate an intimate atmosphere. Buy dessert if you must. A little bit of foresight for the details will help enormously.

- Because you are entertaining business colleagues and many people have a hard time talking about anything but business in those contexts, make an effort to change the subject away from office matters. Ask about vacation plans or hobbies or introduce a non sequitur, such as, "If it were your birthday, what would you like for dinner?" I confess I wasn't always fully successful at this, though I hope the guests forgave an inevitable side moment of tête-à-tête shop-talk. Perhaps a *soupçon* of business helps emphasize the pleasure balance.

PRELIMINARIES

BEFORE-DINNER DRINKS: The meet-and-greet cocktail hour can be as simple as a glass of wine or Champagne and water or light juices for guests who prefer nonalcoholic drinks or as elaborate as the occasion demands (perhaps requiring a bar with all the paraphernalia to accommodate trendy, high-cal pastel-colored mixed drinks—but unless mixology is your hobby, who has the time for that on top of entertaining your guests and preparing dinner?). Match the before-dinner drinks with the guests. If you know the most important guest's preference, serve it. But I vote for simple and moderate if you are about to serve a meal. And, of course, always offer a little food—finger food is right—whenever you serve alcoholic beverages. Once in a while we throw a large cocktail party (without cocktails) in our home to see a lot of people at once. Last summer we managed two in the same month, one in New York and one in Provence. We had a lot of people stop by in New York, where we offered rosé Champagne, red wine, or water with finger foods. No one took up the red wine, everyone tried the Champagne, often repeatedly, and a few people stayed with or switched to water. In Provence, we offered rosé wine, pastis (the local anise-based alcoholic drink specialty, which also exists in a pleasing nonalcoholic version), and water. No problem. Everyone was there for a good time, seemingly had a good time, and did not miss the drinks we did not offer. The point is, don't worry about what you don't have to serve (what, no thirty-year-old single malt?). Serve something pleasing and move on.

SETTING THE TABLE: In my home, when it comes to dinnerware, formal is out, casual is in. Use what you have. I never bought a complete set of china, and during all my continuing years entertaining in New York, I used different dishes for each course, mixing white and color, porcelain and clay ceramics. In some cases I didn't have enough of one color or design plate for everyone, and so played with one type for women and another for men. Always a topic of conversation. Remember to "plate" your food so it is attractive and inviting. I also use a three-color rule for the main course, which ensures a colorful array of food as well as a balanced meal. Plus, fitting three foods—say, meat or fish and two vegetables—on a plate means your portions are not supersize.

NAPKINS, GLASSWARE, CUTLERY: Paper cocktail napkins come in all colors and shapes and themes and work well for premeal drinks, but when it comes to dining, cloth napkins are a must. A white linen one always looks great and will go with any type and color of dishes. Today, many hostesses like place mats instead of tablecloths, especially when the tables are modern ones, and with glass tops no tablecloth is fine. For lunch, the napkin should be at the center of the plate, whereas for dinner it should be to the left of the dish. The glass placement: Farthest to the left is the water glass, next the white, then the red. A single good, inexpensive wineglass works for everything. Not enough silverware for every course? Not to worry. If necessary, tell your guests to keep their knife and fork (if you only set one of each they'll get the idea anyway). Otherwise, set the forks on the left and knives on the right and work your way from the outside to the inside for each course you are planning to serve.

SEATING AND DECORUM: Good table manners will never go out of style. Not all of us are perfect hostesses, and a whole book on table manners and the art of entertaining can be daunting to read. Nowadays there is greater flexibility, yet so many of us are intimidated when it comes to entertaining with style. In my world of "less is more," here are a few practices I apply.

For seating, it is a function of the type of guests you will be welcoming and should be planned ahead; making sure that guests will have a good time should be the main objective. If the boss and spouse come to dinner and it's the first time, and if the boss is male, sit him on your right. If it's a female, seat her at the right of your spouse or partner.

If they've already been guests in your home, the oldest or highest-ranking woman sits next to your partner. But rules and conventions are made to be broken. Breaking spouses up has become accepted, even preferred, seating, though it depends on the couple. Balance the shy girl with an outgoing guy. (Remember the golden rule of party conversation: Don't wait to be asked a question. Be the one who lets your neighbor have fun and be attentive.) For more than six to eight guests, use place cards to simplify your life when dinner is announced. By the way, it is generally a good idea not to invite other business colleagues when you invite your boss. You are after all working on relationship building, so focus.

Seating arrangements vary with cultures. In the United

States, the host and hostess tend to head the table. In France they tend to be in the middle. In Morocco you sit on the floor and eat with your fingers. Read about basic rules before visiting a country. I remember vividly one of my first lunch attendances at a château in Champagne. After being served the first asparagus of the season as an appetizer, two young men—right out of a scene from a comedy—drank the content of their *rince-doigts* (finger bowls), to our stupefaction. Lesson: If you don't know what to do with a utensil, check the hostess and mimic. Remember the scene in the French restaurant in *Pretty Woman* when the character played by Julia Roberts eats snails for the first time? Well, it is probably a good idea not to serve snails or something that requires a finger bowl at a business dinner at home.

One little piece of dying table-and-utensil etiquette that I value but they don't teach at drama school is laying your knife and fork on your plate at the five o'clock position to signal to the host or waiter that you have finished eating what is on your dish. I expect that when I leave this earth, I may well have been the last person to remember this nicety (unless you pass it on).

MOOD AND AMBIANCE: Having grown up in a flower-loving family, I can't imagine hosting a party and not having flowers. They sing "welcome" even if only from a small vase with a few freesias, ranunculus, anemones, or sweet peas. Avoid lavish flowers (especially scented ones) on the dining room table, as they are not too friendly with the aromas of wines. And tall arrangements can cut into eye contact across the table. Save a branch of scented flowers such as lilacs or peonies for the bathroom or the entrance. Lighting is important, and a few unscented candles can create a soothing atmosphere, but don't overdo it. Soft lighting flatters people's faces. Music is a tricky subject. For a small dinner party, it's not necessary and for a large group it still should be more background than what you hear in many noisy restaurants where it seems they don't want people to talk, or maybe they want to sell extra drinks to keep customers' throats wet!

GIFTS AND SURPRISES: Don't be surprised if your gift for inviting someone to your home is a reciprocal invitation. Be forewarned. That used to be the rule in France, and indeed became almost a deterrent to home entertaining. We like to give more than we receive, entertain more than be entertained, and who has the time or wants to feel obliged to attend a repeat engagement or many repeat engagements (not that they won't be enjoyable or good relationship building)? Still, today when people in many cultures no longer feel obliged to exchange your "gift" with a similar one, if people have a good time, they often will seek to get together again, whether at home or at a restaurant or event. So, entertain and you are in play.

If you are invited to someone's home for the first time, I suggest that the day before you send some white flowers with a little "looking forward to tomorrow" note and, depending on the person and occasion, perhaps a business card. A round floral arrangement is best because it fits anywhere. As for the color of the flowers, white goes with any type of decoration; however, remember to be culturally sensitive to the color and type of flower. (White flowers, for instance, evoke funerals in some Pacific Rim and Muslim countries.) If you don't want to or forgot to send flowers beforehand, do send them afterward, with a handwritten note thanking your host. Though a common practice, it is never the best move to bring cut flowers to a dinner party, as the last thing a hostess needs is to have to look for an appropriate vase and take time to arrange them instead of spending time with the guests or preparing the meal. And, of course, the well-prepared hostess already has all the flowers around the home she feels are appropriate. If you've entertained, you know what sort of thank-you gifts are most welcome, perhaps a bottle of Champagne or wine, teas, chocolate—and if you know your hosts a bit better it could be a book, a CD, some perfume, something for the kitchen or the garden, or something unusual that speaks your brand without selling it.

．．．．．．．．．．．．．．．．．

COOKING AND MENUS

Making a meal is an art that anyone can master. No genius neurons necessary. And you don't need to be an accomplished chef to put out an exciting, elegant, delicious meal. A short but foolproof and practiced repertoire is all one needs, as in three tested dinner menus for entertainment purposes. Practice is the essential ingredient in cooking well or learning to cook, though a requirement is a desire to cook and please; other keys to success are planning, good organization, respect for the seasons and for the simplicity principle (no recipe with twenty-eight ingredients, eight pieces of fancy equipment required, or six hours of sweat in the kitchen), and calm (for the essential "seasoning" ingredient, read "stressless"). And no experimenting on guests.

I have a couple of other rules for "entertainment" cooking: The dishes have to be simple, which means a short list of ingredients that are easily and quickly put together, and the cooking either has to be fast and last-minute (anything *"en papillote"*—cooked in the oven in its juices within a parchment paper envelope—works well) or long and slow so it is literally just taken out of the oven as guests arrive and doesn't take you away from the guests and the table during dinner.

People find lots of reasons not to cook and entertain at home, from lack of confidence to lack of time to their not having all the pots, plates, knives, utensils, and gadgets they see on cooking shows on TV (mostly entertainment). Ban the excuses. Again, what is the worst thing that can happen? If the dish you prepare is not perfect, don't apologize. As a matter of fact, apologies draw attention to hitherto unnoticed flaws, are often unnecessary, and can make things worse. I have witnessed this countless times in business at every level. For example, at a staff presentation or a major speaking engagement, one sort of apology goes something like this: "I am sorry but I'm very nervous speaking in public" or "this is my first presentation, and I am sorry if . . ." Do men ever apologize? It reminds me of my friend Helen, who makes a delicious paella, and once she brought it to the table and said, "Sorry, my friends, it just occurred to me I left out the lobster." She did indeed forget it, but did she need to say it? No. Most paellas don't call for lobster (high cost, anyone?), and hers was a seafood paella and had plenty of good stuff, so her apology was inappropriate to all but her. It's a woman thing, isn't it? Make do with what you have.

Rita, on the other hand, handled a "disaster" splendidly. She had invited friends to her home for a chocolate fondue after her daughter's concert. Everything was ready for the celebration. She had spent a few hours that morning precutting the various fruits and arranging them on a large platter and even melted the chocolate so that when they returned home with the guests, all she would have to do was take the fruit platter out and put the chocolate in the fondue fountain contraption. She had done it before, and it had been a big success. This time, however, her teenage son helped out, and, yes, he didn't assemble the pieces correctly, and when she started the fountain—I am not making this up—a sort of chocolate fireworks took place in front of the guests. Luckily, only Rita and her son were covered with chocolate, if you don't count the huge table and tablecloth, and it took a few seconds (which felt like eternity, she said) to stop the machine. At that point everybody was laughing to tears. Rita, being Rita, didn't lose her aplomb but said, "Now that the show is over, let's have the real thing," went to the kitchen, grabbed more chocolate slabs, fixed the machine (recognizing that a piece had been screwed in upside down), and made her fondue. I call that grace under fire. The party was a success.

. . . .

SIGNATURE MEALS

What and how you choose to serve guests says a lot about you. It becomes part of your brand. So, what's your signature dish or two? Is it something you cook or is it part of your family tradition, say Grandma T's apple crumble or Aunt D's pot roast or Mom's *spaghetti alle vongole*? Perhaps you have a version of a dish you enjoyed at some special restaurant or on some special occasion? Consider including it in your business meal cooked at home. Personalize the menus or offer or develop your own to reflect your style and personality. Always include a dish you can speak about engagingly, albeit briefly. Have a story to tell about it.

For these sample menus that follow, I did not include hors d'oeuvres, as I usually choose to serve a glass of Champagne or white wine with a tray of either olives, slivers of Parmesan, various nuts, or some thin salami slices, perhaps grizzini wrapped with razor-thin slices of prosciutto, or some delicate cheese sticks from a gourmet grocery. So, I don't need to worry about replenishing, preparing, or warming at that stage and can devote my time to my guests or last-minute dinner prep. Occasionally, for a very special occasion, I'll make *gougères* (the delicious little cheese puffs), as they are to my mind the perfect accompaniment to Champagne, but they are highly addictive. I like to serve just enough food before sitting down at the dining room table so as not to drink on an empty stomach. If I am going to serve an extra course, I'd rather it be a cheese course toward the end of the meal, in the French fashion—usually three slivers with a slice of olive or walnut bread. With the range of international cheeses and great breads available in America, guests always seem to enjoy discovering yet another variety.

TOUT AU CHOCOLAT

I don't need to be convinced that nine out of ten love or like chocolate . . . and, yes, the tenth one is (probably) lying (a line I've used often to smiles and laughter). A dinner with chocolate throughout is an attention grabber and this one is delicious. It is great for chocoholics, Valentine's Day, and even to introduce duck to a reluctant someone. I guarantee your boss will remember it.

APPETIZER: Chestnut Velouté (soup) au Chocolat

MAIN COURSE: Duck Breasts with Apples and Chocolate Sauce

DESSERT: Mousse au Chocolat with Ginger

SIDE DISH(ES): With the duck, serve green peas (use frozen or fresh) in small side-dish bowls, or perhaps a special vegetable in your own style.

WINE: A medium- to full-bodied red would work fine throughout this meal. Cabernet sauvignon has an affinity with chocolate, so a Californian or Chilean cab or a Bordeaux would be my pick . . . nothing too hard, though. If you want to splurge on a glass of dessert wine, any orange Muscat-based sweet wine, such as Muscat Beaumes-de-Venise, will marry well with chocolate, as will a Banyuls. And so will a nice Cognac.

CHESTNUT VELOUTÉ AU CHOCOLAT

SERVES 4

1 pound peeled chestnuts (jars of peeled chestnuts are available at many grocery stores)

2 to 3 cups vegetable stock (beef stock is fine, too)

1/2 cup heavy cream

2 teaspoons sour cream or crème fraîche

Salt and freshly ground pepper

Small square of dark chocolate (over 60% cacao) or cocoa powder for garnish

1. Put the peeled chestnuts in a saucepan with 2 cups of stock. Bring to a simmer, uncovered, and cook for 45 minutes, adding more stock if necessary to keep the chestnuts covered.

2. When the chestnuts are tender, drain, reserving the stock. Purée the chestnuts in a food processor or blender. Return the puréed chestnuts to the reserved stock, stirring, and add the heavy cream and cook a few more minutes till hot. Season to taste.

3. Serve in individual bowls and add a dollop of crème fraîche or sour cream in the middle. Grate dark chocolate on top or dust with cocoa powder.

NOTE: *The bulk of the work, steps 1 and 2, can be completed a day ahead. Reheat before serving.*

DUCK BREASTS WITH APPLES
AND CHOCOLATE SAUCE

SERVES 4

2 duck breasts

2 tablespoons red wine vinegar

2 tablespoons chicken or veal stock

2 tablespoons water

2 ounces dark chocolate (over 60% cacao), cut into small pieces

2 Granny Smith apples

Salt and freshly ground pepper

1. Bring duck breasts to room temperature and score them (make shallow crisscross slices in the skin, almost scratches) so fat can render during cooking. Sear in a warm skillet over medium-high heat, skin side down first, for about 5 to 7 minutes on each side. Set aside on a warm dish and cover with foil.

2. Deglaze the duck fat in the pan by adding the vinegar. Then add stock, water, and chocolate pieces. Continue cooking over low heat until chocolate has melted. Season to taste.

3. Wash and core the apples (keep skin on for crunchiness and color). Cut into quarters, then into fine juliennes.

4. Pour/smear half of the chocolate sauce on each plate and create a pattern of your choice with a spatula or spoon (or your finger). Arrange julienned apples in the middle of each plate. Cut the duck breasts into one-inch slices on a bias and place on top of the apples. Pour the remaining chocolate sauce and serve immediately.

NOTE: *You can replace the apples with Comice pears, as long as they are not too ripe to retain the* craquant, *or crispness that adds to the various textures of the dish.*

MOUSSE AU CHOCOLAT WITH GINGER

SERVES 4

12 ounces dark chocolate (more than
60% cacao preferred), coarsely chopped

8 ½ ounces heavy cream

2 ounces butter

2 egg whites

2 tablespoons sugar

2 ounces ginger confit (available in
gourmet stores), thinly minced

1. Melt the chocolate pieces with 2 ounces of the heavy cream in the top of a double boiler (a pan set over a pan of simmering water) on medium heat. Off the heat, add the butter and stir well—until the texture is smooth.

2. Beat the remaining heavy cream until stiff peaks are formed, then set it aside. Beat the egg whites, adding the sugar bit by bit, until they are firm. Gently fold together the whipped cream and the egg-white mixture, and add 2 tablespoons of the melted chocolate.

3. Add ginger confit to the chocolate mixture and fold in the cream, egg whites, and chocolate mixture.

4. Refrigerate for a minimum of 2 hours.

5. Serve in individual small cups or *verrines* (the famous little glasses used in fancy restaurants for supermini portions of soup, or for *amuse-bouche*).

For a variation, serve the mousse in the center of a dessert plate, and pour mango coulis around it.

You can certainly make this a day ahead; I prefer it that way.

SLOW-COOKED CHICKEN

My cousin Andrée in Aix-en-Provence used to make this dish. The slow cooking and the local sweet wine make it unique and flavorful without being sweet. Then you have some play with your veggies. On cold New York winter nights, I admit that root vegetables (a trilogy of turnip, parsnip, and celeriac) are yummy; and in the spring, carrots and the green celery branches work extremely well. Leftovers are super, so if you have two large pans, make two chickens, and you'll have another meal prepared for two days later. It's good cold, too.

APPETIZER: Tuna Mille-feuille

MAIN COURSE: Chicken Provençal with Muscat Beaumes-de-Venise

DESSERT: Rice Pudding Caroline's Style

SIDE DISH(ES): None.

WINE: Chicken is wine friendly and while a light red is a good choice, with this dish I prefer a soft white, such as a Sancerre. My mother would serve a Riesling from Alsace. You don't need a dessert wine . . . but, since the bottle is open, a sweet Muscat Beaumes-de-Venise, *bien sûr.*

TUNA MILLE-FEUILLE

SERVES 4

3 tablespoons plus 2 teaspoons olive oil

One 12-ounce tuna steak

Salt and pepper

1 red pepper, julienned, steamed (4 minutes), and chilled

1 avocado, peeled and cut into $\frac{1}{4}$-inch pieces

1 mango, peeled and cut into $\frac{1}{4}$-inch pieces

1 teaspoon minced parsley

1 teaspoon minced cilantro

1 teaspoon Dijon mustard

Juice of half of a lemon

1 Granny Smith apple, peeled, quartered, and julienned

1. Heat 2 teaspoons of olive oil in a medium pan over medium-high heat. Season both sides of the tuna steak. When the pan is hot, add tuna and sear about 3 minutes on each side for medium rare. Refrigerate for at least 30 minutes.

2. Mix pepper, avocado, mango, and herbs in a bowl. Season to taste.

3. To make a vinaigrette, whisk together the mustard and lemon juice in a bowl, then add the remaining 3 tablespoons olive oil in a slow stream, whisking until emulsified. Season to taste.

4. To serve, remove tuna from refrigerator, cut into $\frac{1}{2}$-inch pieces, and divide into four portions. Place one portion on each serving plate and shape into a rectangle, about 2 inches by 4 inches. Cover tuna with a layer of the pepper-avocado-mango mixture and top with a layer of apples. Drizzle vinaigrette over and around the mille-feuille and serve at once.

Steps 1 to 3 can be prepared in advance.

CHICKEN PROVENÇAL
WITH MUSCAT BEAUMES-DE-VENISE

SERVES 4

1 chicken (3–3 ½ pounds)
2 tablespoons olive oil
1 teaspoon dried tarragon (or thyme)
Salt and freshly ground pepper

1 cup of medium shallots, peeled and left whole
1 fennel bulb, cut into ½-inch juliennes
1 cup Muscat Beaumes-de-Venise (or other Muscat sweet wine)

1. Preheat oven to 350 degrees.

2. Cut the chicken into four quarters. Toss with the oil and arrange the pieces in a large roasting pan. Sprinkle with tarragon and season to taste. Add the shallots and fennel strips over and in between the chicken pieces. Pour the sweet wine all over.

3. Cover tightly with aluminum foil and cook for 1 hour and 30 minutes. Uncover, baste with the pan juices, and continue cooking for about 15 minutes, until the skin gets lightly brown. Allow it to rest 5 minutes before serving.

RICE PUDDING CAROLINE'S STYLE

SERVES 4

1 quart whole milk

6 ounces short grain or Arborio rice

½ cup minus one tablespoon sugar

1 ounce sweet butter, melted

½ teaspoon cinnamon

Pinch of salt

1. Preheat oven to 350 degrees. Mix all the ingredients together in an ovenproof casserole or soufflé dish with high sides. Stir well.

2. Bake for 2 hours without stirring. When the top is golden, cover with aluminum foil and bake another 15 minutes. Serve directly from dish at room temperature.

NOTE: *If you have some left over or you want to prepare this a day ahead to save time, it can be eaten cold the next day. Different but equally good.*

MEMORY LANE LAMB

Growing up in Eastern France, where pork rules, I didn't often eat lamb except at Easter and occasional meals with family friends, when a leg of lamb was the easy and efficient choice. Once I started to go to Provence on my own to my cousin Andrée's, I learned the Mediterranean way of cooking, and her simple lamb dish was my favorite, as it led to my discovery of basil, which to this day is one of my choice herbs. The fresh, flavorful, powerful basil of Provence is unforgettable. Cousin Andrée also proved to be a great influence on me as a cooking teacher when I was a teenager. My mother taught me to love food and how to eat, but she was such a good cook she did most of the cooking!

APPETIZER: Mackerel en Papillote

MAIN COURSE: Lamb with Tomatoes and Pistou (For entertaining, this dish can be made the day before and reheated.)

DESSERT: Pear en Papillote with Orange Coulis

SIDE DISH(ES): In Provence we enjoyed the lamb dish with polenta, and in Alsace, when my mother duplicated it, she always served it with fettuccine or tagliatelle (Alsatians love pasta with fish and meat). In Paris my godmother served it with *pommes vapeur* (steamed potatoes). In the States I use the small red bliss potatoes. All accompaniments are good, and each brings back different memories from the table.

WINE: The lamb cries out to me for a rich, round, Rhône-style blend. I'd pick a great value Côte-du-Rhône Villages red wine or kick it up a notch with a sublime Châteauneuf-du-Pape.

MACKEREL EN PAPILLOTE

SERVES 4

4 mackerel fillets, 4 ounces each	*1 teaspoon paprika*
2 teaspoons olive oil	*1 tablespoon minced cilantro*
Juice of two limes	*1 tablespoon minced parsley*
1 teaspoon Dijon mustard	*Salt and freshly ground pepper*

1. Preheat the oven to 350 degrees. Cut 8 pieces of parchment paper into squares large enough to cover each mackerel fillet and leave a 2-inch border all along. Lightly brush 4 pieces of the paper with olive oil. Put each fillet in the center of each parchment paper.

2. Whisk together lime juice, mustard, and paprika and pour over each fillet. Sprinkle with cilantro and parsley and season to taste. Place the remaining parchment papers on the tops and fold up the edges to form packets.

3. Put the papillotes on a baking sheet and bake for 8 to 9 minutes (the fish is cooked when the top of the parchment paper is hot). Set each papillote on a plate and serve immediately. Let your guests open their packets and spoon the juices over the fish.

LAMB WITH TOMATOES AND PISTOU

SERVES 4

2 tablespoons olive oil

3–4 pounds boned lamb shoulder, cut into 2 ½-inch squares

2 pounds tomatoes, coarsely chopped

1 head garlic, peeled and sliced

1 bay leaf

1 teaspoon thyme

Pinch of sugar

2 tablespoons water

Salt and freshly ground pepper

¼ cup shirred fresh basil leaves

1. You'll need a cast-iron skillet with a lid. Heat the olive oil in the skillet over medium heat, then add the lamb pieces. Cook, stirring, until all the meat is brown. Add the tomatoes, garlic, bay leaf, thyme, sugar, and water. Season to taste.

2. Bring to a simmer, cover, and cook over low heat for 1 ½ hours, stirring occasionally.

3. When the meat is very tender, sprinkle with basil, stir well, and serve immediately.

PEAR EN PAPILLOTE WITH ORANGE COULIS

SERVES 4

4 pears (Williams work well with their tender meat)

4 lemon slices

1 teaspoon butter

2 oranges, including zest

½ teaspoon orange flower water

1. Preheat oven to 350 degrees. Peel the pears, keeping them whole and the stem on. Gently rub a slice of lemon on each pear. Place each pear on a buttered 10-inch square of aluminum foil.

2. Grate 2 tablespoons of orange zest and sprinkle over pears. Close the papillotes, using a toothpick to secure. Bake for 15 minutes.

3. Slice both ends off both oranges. Place fruit on a work surface and with paring knife remove peel and pith in a single curved motion, following the shape of the fruit. Working over a bowl to catch the juices, slice between sections to remove whole segments. Add orange flower water.

4. When pears are done, open the papillotes and pour the orange coulis over. Serve immediately.

MAKING IT

"Making it" is a climb, no question, but where you get off can be your choice. In Manhattan we live on the top of a fifteen-story apartment building. I often walk the stairs for exercise (which takes no longer than the elevator making a couple of stops). I've "made it" when I reach the top. Some days I do it more than once, some days not at all. Other days, when I have been away and not up to the stair routine or am simply "walked out," I climb to the eighth floor and take the elevator the rest of the way. I feel good reaching my eighth-floor goal. The approach is the same; just the stopping-off point is different.

In climbing the career ladder, I never thought about which floor would constitute "making it." Did I feel as if I had made it when I was promoted to president and CEO? No, at least not at the beginning. As an author, when *French Women Don't Get Fat* became a number one *New York Times* bestseller? No. I mean, I had written one book. I was proud and happy, of course, but did not think I had reached some top step or earned a reward. Curiously, looking back now for a moment in my career when I felt I had made it, I am drawn to something early in my tenure with Veuve Clicquot that I mentioned in the introduction—Count Alain de Vogüé absentmindedly calling me Madame Clicquot. It was an unintentional sign of acceptance and respect that meant a lot to me, and at that stage of my career was a sign I had reached a level of accomplishment I had not imagined earlier. I felt flattered, rewarded, and motivated.

How do you manage to make good things happen in your career and in business? I am often asked for advice from women on how to succeed in business and rise in the corporate culture. There's no universal recipe, though there are some common ingredients. Women in their twenties and thirties are frequently overwhelmed by figuring out how to have it all or how to get from A to CEO in this lifetime. (Remember, you can stop off along the way; this is a book for women of all ages and stages.) Women in their forties often puzzle over what they have not done right and what stock they must take in themselves so as not to be passed over into oblivion. People want simple answers, but a lot of simple answers—take this book—add up to a complex mosaic of behaviors and talents.

Educational psychologists tell us it helps for us to receive information three times (sometimes through different inputs, e.g., visual, aural) for us to learn it. Put into practice, that sometimes results in what public speakers are coached to do and what junior high composition teachers preach: Tell them what you are going to tell them, tell them, and tell them what you told them.

Well, good communicators learn to do that in a variety of ways—not always direct; not always verbatim—but most good communicators do indeed do it. Here's how I repeat some key lessons I've learned from answering the question about making good things happen in your career and in business. (I am not reducing the book or summing it up, of course, just extracting one series of ideas that string together.)

1. *Don't be afraid to take risks.* What's the worst thing that can happen? Nothing so bad it can't be fixed when you are in your twenties, thirties, even forties (as long as it is legal . . .). Nothing begets nothing. I left a terrific PR job for a start-up for Veuve Clicquot in the United States. Lots of people thought the move was dumb and that the VCP concept was wrong. I didn't . . . and what did I have to lose? Anyway, I made the concept work: I wrote the marketing plan, hired the most talented people (at least 50 percent women), and with some good timing and, well, brilliant results, lots of fun followed.

2. If necessary, *fire your boss and hook your star to a talented and dynamic leader.* S/he will take you upward with them, inside or outside your current firm, and protect you and nurture you as you continue to make him or her look good. Trust is something most

valued in employees. If you have the rising star's trust, maintain it. It is a great insurance policy. And someday that boss will help you land on your feet comfortably somewhere. First, though, you have to be able to identify and work for a star in however large or small a constellation. If that's not your current boss . . . hint, hint.

3. *Find something you are passionate about* so it doesn't always feel like work, but remember that life is lived in episodes and stages and that passions change. (Note the divorce rate.) The passion thing is not as simple as it appears; there are old passions and there are new passions, as I noted. Again, I was trained as an interpreter but made the decision that food, wine, travel, and associated cultures were what I truly enjoyed and took a relatively entry-level position to get started in a new field (one giant step back, then a great leap forward).

4. Especially as women, you have to *work harder and smarter than everyone else* to succeed and be respected. That's earning it the old-fashioned way. I put in the hours in a mostly man's world. There aren't many shortcuts on the way up. You may hear about one or two people who rocketed because they are special, but they are very rare or work at Internet companies. You can play politics to get ahead, but the safest way to get noticed is to do outstanding work. In America,

meritocracy is the savior for women, though it does not crush all barriers.

5. *Timing is everything . . . make it work for you.* Sometimes you can control the timing of things, often not. What you can do is be sensitive to the timing of your actions. Sometimes it is simply the wrong day or month to ask for a raise. Sometimes that next promotion has to wait for you to get more gray hair. Sometimes that brilliant idea is ahead of its time. The success of *French Women Don't Get Fat* was all about timing. I had the idea twenty years earlier, but sat on it until I thought it was the right time to publish. I don't believe the timing would be as good today, just a few years later, even though the ideas are equally or more relevant. What you need to do is prepare yourself to be in the right place at the right time to seize those great moments of opportunity when they arise and the timing seems right.

6. *Work for a winning company.* Weak or failing companies can have good employees, but would you or anyone rather hire them or someone from a highly successful company? Most often the latter candidate wins. A good employment history opens doors. Be proud to list the places where you have worked on your résumé. During the first half of your career, get a local or global name brand in your profile. It is a permanent reference and is an achievable goal over a

relatively short time. You'll have to face the sober reality of your current company and position, and if necessary take your cues from it.

7. *Follow the money positions.* If you aspire to reach one of the "C" offices (CEO, COO, CFO), you'll need to move out of traditional women's support staff service positions in HR or communications and elsewhere, which dead-end at a vice-presidency. There's nothing wrong with aspiring to be the vice president for corporate communications, it's a great career, but to get to the true power circle and the serious big bucks, you'll need some experience and credibility in line positions with direct P&L and revenue accountability.

8. *Being in the right place at the right time is part luck and part making your own luck.* Being a French woman in New York certainly helped me. Working as a woman in business in the States instead of France helped me. And being a French businesswoman in the States working in the luxury sector certainly was the right fit for me. British accents work well in America. Perhaps better than in England. Work with who you are to align your inherent strengths with your aspirations. If you are an accountant or financial analyst with strong math abilities, that's a pretty strong asset to begin with. What sort of company do you want to work for and where? Position yourself for that op-

portunity. Hard work, knowing yourself, skill, and seizing opportunities at the right time are all part of making your own luck.

9. *Live a balanced life.* You cannot have it all or do it all, at least not at the same time. Recognize that an unhappy personal life often carries over into job performance. Taking care of your mental and physical health is just as important as any career move or responsibility, generally more so. Learn to manage your expectations and live *bien dans sa peau.*

10. Remember, image, image, image . . . *Cultivate your professional image.* Good communication skills are key, and not just a good accent. But I have to be frank, as a woman your image is perceived as more than the quality of your reports or presentations or thinking. Your looks count. How you dress, how you are groomed, how you present yourself, and more. The harsh reality is that women are judged by their looks and men mostly are not. You don't have to be a beauty but you have to be appropriate to your industry. In the luxury goods business, you have to live the brand. Walk into an Armani store and take a look at the employees. But the luxury or fashion business isn't for everyone. Simply work with who you are and what you've got, then work on your image and align it with who you realistically want to be. There's truth in the adage about dressing for the job you want

(as in the next job, not ultimate position) rather than the job you have.

11. Finally, as you know, results rule in the business world, so the key to my success was *beating all the success metrics each year*—sales, revenues, placements, image, et cetera. Beat the projections year after year and you get noticed. And you get promoted on merit. A tip, though, is to be careful not to set yourself up for failure by promising more than you can deliver. Set aggressive but achievable results. My team delivered double-digit growth year after year . . . and outperformed the market year after year. That's how you keep your job and how you keep yourself in Champagne.

I set out to write a book that could help women navigate the steps and paths appropriate to a twenty-first-century work-life style. I hope the ideas and stories in it stimulated you to better "know thyself," and to become better equipped to achieve pleasure, balance, and "success" in business and life at whatever stage you are. If so, I am happy for you and grateful to have had the privilege of supporting you. *Bon courage.*

REMERCIEMENTS

Anyone who has worked for a corporation or agency knows that results are achieved collaboratively, by a team and not a person. Some people earn more credit than others, at times deservedly so, but single-handed achievement is more surface than substance and is rare indeed in business. I have been blessed in both business and in life by being surrounded by gifted collaborators and at times co-conspirators. Thank you all.

Foremost among my team has been and continues to be Edward. He has been there sharing ideas and experiences with me for most of my adult life. Thankfully, we have not yet reached the point of finishing each other's sentences, but after all those conversations around the dinner table, during long walks, plane delays, and much more, it is sometimes hard to remember the origin of my now firmly held and felt beliefs. I thank him for sharing, helping me to develop my ideas, and credit him for some of the "same" ideas that appear in this book. I forgive him for not agreeing with everything I wrote (ah, men) and celebrate his discourse that still has the ability to startle me with brilliant ideas, laughs, and language. The experience of his mind has been and continues to be a profound joy. (And I suppose I should thank New York Institute of Technology, where he is president, for sharing him with me.) Much love and thanks.

Soon someone will likely be able to do a computer search of all the acknowledgment pages in books by major publishers over the last couple of decades. It would not surprise me at all if the name that appeared most frequently is Kathy Robbins, literary agent both astonishing and *bien dans sa peau*. Who imagined I could have my pick of publishers, find the right one for my ideas, and envision editions in a couple of dozen languages? She did, and delivered more and more, time and time again. I value her friendship and support as much as her skills. To the entire team at The Robbins Office goes much appreciation for now years of invaluable aid and collaboration (as well as a bit of conspiracy). They deserve much credit for this volume.

When I said I wanted to write a business book of a different kind, Kathy suggested Peter Borland as the editor, and working with him has proven to be exceedingly easy, efficient, and friendly. As editorial director of Simon & Schuster's Atria Books, he self-effacingly describes himself as a "breakfast, lunch, and dinner" kind of editor, meaning in part he likes good nourishment logically organized in well-shaped units and presented in a clear sequence. As I said well before meeting Peter, breakfast, lunch, and dinner are my favorite pastimes. And Peter cooks a good book. Credit Peter for making this book much better than the outcomes of my first recipe. Blame me for what you do not fancy. Thank you, thank you, Peter, as well as Carolyn Reidy, president and CEO of Simon & Schuster, Judith Curr, executive VP and publisher of Atria Books, and the entire team at Atria for their belief in and enthusiasm for this project as well as their exceptional skills in helping bring it to life.

Erin Jones, Todi Gutman, and Rachelle Bergstein all read multiple versions of the manuscript, and I have profited from their helpful takes on its potency and prose. Their enthusiasm also provided me with periodic boosts along the way. I also owe a sincere debt of gratitude to the outstanding professionals at Alfred A. Knopf, publisher of my two French women books (and the related paperback publisher, Vintage Books). They took an unpublished book author and shepherded her through the twists and turns of a truly bizarre process and industry. Their collaboration made this book possible. R. "Nick" Nichols, gifted illustrator of all my books, once again thank you for making what I do all the more attractive.

And this book certainly could not have been possible without all the people I worked for or with over my career. Thanks for tolerating and perhaps even enjoying me. I learned most things from others and am grateful for the successive teams at Champagne Veuve Clicquot who took a chance on me, then listened to me and took a chance on implementing my ideas. I am greatly appreciative of the experience and exposure my years working for VCP and the larger LVMH group afforded me.

What a parade of characters, challenges, qualities, and celebrations.

Enfin, thank you to all the readers and others who asked for and encouraged me to write this book. I am deeply touched by all those who have taken the time to read and care about my stories and what I have to say. It is the ultimate compliment.

Merci infiniment.

INDEX